Also by Laurence Steinberg

CROSSING PATHS: HOW YOUR CHILD'S ADOLESCENCE
TRIGGERS YOUR OWN CRISIS
ADOLESCENCE
(WITH WENDY STEINBERG)

YOU AND YOUR ADOLESCENT: A PARENT'S GUIDE
FOR AGES 10 TO 20
(WITH ANN LEVINE)

WHEN TEENAGERS WORK: THE PSYCHOLOGICAL AND
SOCIAL COSTS OF ADOLESCENT EMPLOYMENT
(WITH ELLEN GREENBERGER)

Laurence Steinberg, Ph.D.

with

B. Bradford Brown, Ph.D., and

Sanford M. Dornbusch, Ph.D.

SIMON & SCHUSTER

New York   London   Toronto   Sydney   Tokyo   Singapore

BEYOND

THE

CLASSROOM

WHY SCHOOL REFORM

HAS FAILED AND WHAT PARENTS

NEED TO DO

SIMON & SCHUSTER
Rockefeller Center
1230 Avenue of the Americas
New York, NY 10020

Designed by Jennifer Ann Daddio

Manufactured in the United States of America

1   3   5   7   9   10   8   6   4   2

Library of Congress Cataloging-in-Publication Data
Steinberg, Laurence D., date.
Beyond the classroom : why school reform has failed and what parents need to do /
Laurence Steinberg, with B. Bradford Brown and Sanford M. Dornbusch.
p.   cm.
Includes bibliographical references and index.
1. High school students—United States—Social conditions—Longitudinal studies.
2. Academic achievement—United States—Longitudinal studies.   3. Home and school—
United States—Longitudinal studies.   4. High school students—United States—
Attitudes—Longitudinal studies.   I. Brown, B. Bradford (Benson Bradford), date.
II. Dornbusch, Sanford M.   III. Title.
LC205.S74   1996
370.19'342'09794—dc20   96-3662   CIP
ISBN 0-684-80008-X

Acknowledgments

This book is based on an extensive program of research conducted over the past ten years. During that time period, we surveyed more than 20,000 teenagers from nine high schools and spoke with hundreds of their parents and dozens of their teachers. We could not have completed the research for this study without the cooperation of the students, parents, teachers, and administrators who generously gave us their time. To all of these individuals we owe our deepest thanks.

The project was a collaborative effort that involved three universities and research teams. The coauthors of this volume shared equal responsibility for designing and directing the research and for the preparation of numerous scholarly research reports based on the project. In order to give this volume—the first comprehensive presentation of our findings written for a general audience—a single "voice," one of us took primary responsibility for drafting the manuscript. This was entirely a stylistic decision, however; the ideas presented in this book are shared ones that grew out of a close, decade-long collaboration.

Over the course of this study, we had the good fortune of working with a team of exceptionally talented and diligent data analysts and research assistants, including Karen Bogenschneider, Elizabeth Cauffman, Zeng-yin Chen, Michelle Christensen, Randi Cohen, Nancy Darling, Julie Elworth, Suzanne Fegley, Anne Fletcher, Lori Folgert, Rita Ghatak, Kristan Glasgow, Marc Hanellin, Melissa Herman, Jerald Herting, Bih-Hui Huang, Nancy Kaczmarek, Elizabeth Kraemer, Elaina Kyrouz, Cary Lazarro, I-Chun Lin, Randy Mont-Reynaud, Jeanne Barr Morley, Margaret Mory, Nina Mounts, Mark Philipp, Diane Randall, Ricardo Stanton-Salazar, Lisa Troyer, Angela Valenzuela, Pamela B.Vergun, Patricia Weaver, and Kenneth D. Wood. We are especially indebted to our project directors, Susie Lamborn and Phil Ritter, who oversaw the day-to-day operations of the research project, coordinated our staffs, and contributed in many important ways to the study's conceptualization.

In the process of preparing reports of our work for publication in professional journals, we consulted with many colleagues across the country whose wisdom and expertise stimulated and improved our thinking. We are grateful to Oliver Moles, Tommy Tomlinson, P. Herbert Liederman, Urie Bronfenbrenner, Fred Newmann, Thomas Berndt, JoMills Braddock, Layli Phillips, Ellen Greenberger, Diana Baumrind, and Russell Rumberger. Our editor at Simon & Schuster, Bob Bender, carefully critiqued our writing and our thinking, and his suggestions and recommendations improved both tremendously. We are also grateful to our agent, Barbara Lowenstein.

An intensive longitudinal study involving nine research sites and thousands of participants comes with a large price tag. We gratefully acknowledge the financial generosity of the following organizations, without whose support this work would not have been possible: the William T. Grant Foundation, the Spencer Foundation, the Office of Educational Research and Improvement of the U.S. Department of Education, the Lilly Endowment, the Carnegie Corporation of New York.

Finally, many thanks to our families for their love and support.

Laurence Steinberg
Bradford Brown
Sanford M. Dornbusch

Contents

ONE: THE REAL PROBLEM   11

TWO: A NATION AT RISK, A NATION IN DENIAL   29

THREE: SCHOOL REFORM IS NOT THE SOLUTION   47

FOUR: DISENGAGED STUDENTS   62

FIVE: ETHNICITY AND ADOLESCENT ACHIEVEMENT   78

SIX: THE POWER OF AUTHORITATIVE PARENTING   101

SEVEN: THE HOME ENVIRONMENT OF ACADEMICALLY
SUCCESSFUL STUDENTS   122

EIGHT: THE POWER OF PEERS   138

Contents

NINE: ALL WORK AND ALL PLAY MAKES JACK
A DUMB BOY   163

TEN: BEYOND THE CLASSROOM   183

Appendix   195
Notes   202
Bibliography   210
Index   215

ONE

The Real Problem

Some sixty miles west of Philadelphia, in Hershey, Pennsylvania, the Derry Township School Board faced a problem. Severe winter storms had forced the board to cancel school too many times in January and February. After considering a number of alternative plans, the school board decided to add extra days of school in June in order to adhere to the district's 183-day calendar.

This seems like a reasonable solution. But when the district's plan was announced publicly, the township's middle school students walked out in protest. Here is an account of the event, as reported on the front page of the April 7, 1994, *Hershey Chronicle*:

> Nearly a hundred students walked out of the M. S. Hershey Middle School Monday afternoon in protest against a Derry Township School Board decision last week to extend their classes until June 23.
>
> Chanting "Hell no, we won't go," a slogan some of their parents' generation made popular in the 60s during demonstrations against the Vietnam War, the students marched four blocks to Hershey High School shortly before 1 p.m. . . . Most of the students behaved themselves during

the march to and from the high school but a few were observed kicking the garbage cans along the route of Java Avenue. Others climbed on cars parked along the street, and a few attempted to block traffic. . . . [T]he 45-minute protest ended abruptly, when the high school's head football coach, Bob "Gump" May stood his ground at the entrance [to the high school] and declared, "You aren't going in here."

"It's not fair; we have no say," eighth-grader Jill Cottonaso complained. . . .

[One] parent on the scene was Judy Glenn, who said her daughter is a middle school student. "The bottom line is they don't want to go to school until [June] 23rd," Glenn said. "They're good kids," she observed, "but they just wanted to make a statement."

On its own, the 1994 student walkout in Hershey is not especially newsworthy—no one was injured, no property was damaged, the incident was over in less than an hour. But to my mind, what is most interesting about the Hershey student protest is that it could have happened in any school district in the United States—rich or poor, urban, rural, or suburban. To be sure, we would not expect even middle-class adolescents to jump for joy at the prospect of a slightly lengthened school year—our son, Ben, whose parents are clearly committed to education, listened to the radio announcements of school closings during the 1994 winter with a mile-wide grin on his face. But young adolescents staging a demonstration against making up school days lost to bad weather? In past eras, students would never have publicly protested such a decision. And, needless to say, such a protest today would be unheard of in most other parts of the world.

That middle school students—eleven-, twelve-, and thirteen-year-olds—would walk out of school to protest these additional instructional days is symbolic of a deep and profound problem in our children's and our own attitudes toward education. Indeed, in some ways the demonstration is a symptom of a much larger problem in the socialization of young people in the contemporary United States.

As an expert on adolescent development, I pay close attention to the images of young people portrayed in the media. To the extent that popular portrayals of adolescents on television and in film can be taken as evidence of what we *think* our nation's youth are up to, a lack of commitment to school among America's students must be pervasive. For example, on the 1994 tele-

vision series "My So-Called Life," which followed the daily affairs of an intelligent, articulate, middle-class high school sophomore—a thoughtful
show that, interestingly enough, was heralded in the press for its "realistic"
portrayal of adolescent life—classrooms are filled with dozing students
whose heads lie on their desks. Even the simplest questions from teachers are
met with the blank stares of deliberate disenchantment.

Media discussions of the nation's educational shortcomings invariably
emphasize the problems of inner-city schools. Because their difficulties are
so much more severe than are those of suburban schools, and because the
problems are more obviously worrisome—the decrepit state of buildings,
the wildly out-of-date textbooks and antiquated laboratories, the ubiqui-
tousness of violence and drugs—the education of the urban poor understandably commands the lion's share of media attention.

Yet it would be foolish to succumb to the view that America's educational problems are limited to schools in poor neighborhoods or to students
from disadvantaged families. As I make clear in the chapters that follow,
America's educational problems afflict families and communities from all
walks of life. Across the country, whether surrounded by suburban affluence
or urban poverty, students' commitment to school is at an all-time low. And,
as you will read in chapter 2 of this book, American students' low level of
commitment to school is matched by their consistently poor showing on
standardized tests of achievement and knowledge. Today's students know
less, and can do less, than their counterparts twenty-five years ago.

Most people have strong opinions about the "true" causes of the decline
in American student achievement. Some individuals blame our schools and
teachers. Some believe that drugs are the root cause of the problem. Others
point to the "breakdown" of the American family. And still others attack the
mass media. The truth of the matter, though, is that most discussions of
America's educational problems, and how best to address them, are based
more on rhetoric than on rigorous research.

In 1985, my colleagues and I began planning the most extensive study
ever conducted of the forces in youngsters' lives that affect their interest and
performance in school, in an effort to understand what was happening to
American students and why their apparent commitment to school was so
tenuous. Our goal was to describe, in as much detail as possible, the ways in
which parents, peers, and communities influence students' commitment to

school. Our multidisciplinary research team included psychologists, sociologists, psychiatrists, and educational researchers from Stanford University, Temple University, and the University of Wisconsin. Over the course of our research, which took two years of planning and pilot-testing, four years of data collection in the field, and four years of data analysis, we studied more than 20,000 teenagers and their families in nine very different American communities.

The research we carried out differs from previous studies of American education in a number of significant ways. Most important, we deliberately focused our attention outside schools themselves. Given the vast amount of previous research that had already been conducted on effective schools and classrooms—and the absence of any consistently encouraging findings showing that reforming schools or classrooms makes much of a difference in student performance—it made little sense to conduct yet another study of teachers, classrooms, or schools in an effort to understand America's achievement problem and what we might do within schools to address it. Instead of reinventing this wheel, we took a very different approach. We wondered if we might get a better handle on the pervasive problem of poor student achievement and low student commitment by looking at what was taking place not in schools, but in students' homes, in their peer groups, and in their communities.

This book represents the culmination of more than ten years of work by a team of experienced and accomplished social scientists. Over the past decade, we have published many of these findings in scholarly journals aimed at other researchers. In order to keep the technical details at a minimum, I have tried here to tell the story of our research in a language that is unencumbered by the jargon of statistics, research design, and social science. But it is important that readers know that the evidence behind the findings we report here is good science that has been reviewed, critiqued, and found acceptable by other scholars. Readers who are interested in the more technical details of the research, or who wish to read the scientific reports themselves, will find a listing of our project's technical and scholarly publications, as well as details about the study, in the appendix.

STUDYING STUDENT "ENGAGEMENT"

As a social scientist interested in adolescence, I spend a fair amount of time in schools. Whenever I visit a high school or junior high school classroom, I am always struck by the enormous variability in students' behavior and in the expressions on their faces. Some will be actively involved in the class activity, whether listening to a teacher's lecture, participating in a classroom discussion, or busily working on a written assignment. In the same classroom, though—with the same teacher, lesson plan, and instructional techniques—there will likely be just as many students who are not part of the action. Some are daydreaming, staring off into space, their minds far away from the business at hand. Some are sleeping, heads resting atop their desks. Others are busy, but not at the business of school; they are writing letters to friends, drawing sketches in their notebooks, talking with classmates, making plans for the evening or weekend.

One of the goals of our study was to better understand the causes of these differences in student interest. Our research team used the term *engagement* to describe the degree to which students are psychologically "connected" to what is going on in their classes. By engagement, we mean something more than mere interest or commitment—although engaged students are, to be sure, both interested in school and committed to doing well there. When highly engaged students are in class, they are there emotionally as well as physically. They concentrate on the task at hand, they strive to do their best when tested or called upon, and when they are given homework or other outside assignments, they do them on time and in good faith. They participate actively in class discussions, think about the material covered in their courses, and genuinely care about the quality of their work. Disengaged students, in contrast, do only as much as it takes to avoid getting into trouble. They do not exert much effort in the classroom, are easily distracted during class, and expend little energy on in-school or out-of-school assignments. They have a jaded, often cavalier attitude toward education and its importance to their future success or personal development. When disengaged students are in school, they are clearly just going through the motions. When they are not in school, school is the last thing on their mind.

There are many reasons to closely examine the factors that either increase or interfere with youngsters' engagement in school. Because children who are not committed to school do not make good students, and because individuals who are not good students are unlikely as adults to become successful members of a skilled workforce, signs of widespread alienation among students today do not bode well for America's competitiveness in the international marketplace over the coming decades. If we are to be economically competitive later, our children must be committed to school now.

Examining the roots of children's commitment to school is also important for understanding the causes of individual differences in life success *within* the United States. It is really a shame that our culture is so fascinated with stories of individuals who "made it" as adults despite having had poor records of academic achievement as children. Yes, there have been adult millionaires who dropped out of high school, geniuses whose talents were overlooked by their teachers, and successful athletes and actors who, even as adults, can barely read and write. But these stories are exceptions to the rule, and we do our children a disservice by overstating their frequency and maintaining the myths surrounding them. Doing well in school is still one of the best—if not *the* best—predictors of later success, whether measured by the quality or quantity of one's higher education, the prestige of one's occupation, or the income and wealth that one accumulates as an adult. Although there is no magic formula for adult happiness, success in school markedly increases one's chances. Our study helps us understand why some children succeed in school and why others do not, and so helps illuminate the causes of individual differences in adult success.

An examination of youngsters' engagement in school is more than a study of educational achievement or future occupational attainment, however. Our study provides a much larger window on the overall psychological and social health of the nation's children. School is, after all, one of the few responsibilities we expect all youngsters to fulfill, regardless of their background or family origins. It is one of the few goals that parents from all walks of life agree on. As a broad barometer, then, engagement in school is an indicator of children's commitment not only to education, but to the goals and values held by adult society—by their parents, by their teachers, and by members of their community. If children feel negative, or ambivalent, or merely nonchalant about school, this tells us something about their relations with adult society and, as well, about the messages and priorities they are learning from their elders.

Interest in school also is an important indicator of youngsters' well-being, because educational commitment is so highly correlated with other psychological and behavioral indicators of successful functioning. Because school is so central a part of the child's life, engagement there can be a buffer against psychological problems, and disengagement from school often is a symptom of psychological difficulty—in much the same way that satisfaction with work is associated with better mental health among adults, and chronic unemployment with psychological maladjustment. Not surprisingly, then, children who are interested and involved in school score higher on measures of psychological adjustment, such as assessments of self-esteem, responsibility, and competence in social relationships. Conversely, disengagement from school is both a cause and a consequence of psychological and behavioral problems. Children who are alienated from school are far more likely to have psychological problems, ranging from withdrawal and depression to acting out and aggression. As teenagers, youngsters who are disengaged from school are far more likely than their peers to use and abuse drugs and alcohol, fall prey to depression, experiment with early sex, and commit acts of crime and delinquency. For these reasons, understanding the causes and correlates of children's engagement in school helps us better understand the forces in their lives that affect all aspects of their behavior and well-being, not just their performance on tests of school achievement.

In our study, we focused on high school students, for a number of reasons. First, although, as I noted earlier, the problem of poor achievement is not limited to high-school-age students, these youngsters' test scores have received the most attention in both the analyses of the decline in performance over time and in international comparisons. Second, adolescence is a time when most individuals begin making choices about how they will spend their time and prioritize their activities. Because we were interested in learning how adolescents' time out of school affects their experience in school, it was important to focus on an age group in which there would be considerable variation in individuals' behavior. There is far more variability in adolescents' daily experiences than there is in the experiences of elementary school children. Finally, adolescents generally can express their views of their world more adequately than younger children, and understanding youngsters' perceptions is a key to understanding their experiences.

Although our research focus was on adolescents, our findings are important to adults concerned about students of all ages, however. While some of the specific themes explored in this book are clearly more relevant to high school students than to younger ones—the role of extracurricular activities or part-time employment in achievement, for example—the more general points are applicable to families with children of all ages. More important, many of the steps we can take to help adolescents perform better in school, while effective when taken during adolescence, are likely to be even more effective when initiated earlier in a youngster's life. It is never too early to begin doing the things that facilitate success in school.

SOME ALARMING FINDINGS

The picture that emerged from our research was disheartening—alarmingly so. Indeed, I came away from the study feeling that the problems facing our country's educational system—and, consequently, our country itself—are deep, pervasive, and profound. In real life, as on television, America's students are largely disengaged from the serious business of education.

Before you consider each of the following results that emerged from our study, keep in mind that our study focused on youngsters from all walks of life, not just adolescents living in dire poverty, or students identified as "at risk" for some sort of educational problem. Many of the participants in our study were perfectly average or above-average students attending perfectly average or above-average public schools.

Here are some of the things we found:

An extremely high proportion of American high school students do not take school, or their studies, seriously.
- Over one-third of the students we surveyed said that they get through the day in school primarily by "goofing off with their friends."
- Two-thirds of the students in our sample say they cheated on a school test during the past school year. Nearly nine out of ten students in our sample say they copied someone else's homework sometime during the last year.

American students' time out of school is seldom spent in activities that reinforce what they are learning in their classes. More typically, their time and energy is focused on activities that compete with, rather than complement, their studies.

- The average American high school student spends about four hours per week on homework outside of school. In other industrialized countries, the average is about four hours per *day*. Half of all the students in our study reported not doing the homework they are assigned. Fewer than 15 percent of students spend as much as five hours each week reading for pleasure. One-third say they spend five or more hours each week "partying" with their friends.

- Two-thirds of high school students are employed, and half hold down a part-time job that takes up more than fifteen hours weekly. One in six works more than twenty-five hours each week. More than one-third of students who work say they take easier classes so that their job won't hurt their grades.

- Nearly 40 percent of students who participate in a school-sponsored extracurricular activity, usually athletics, say they are often so tired from it that they can't study.

The adolescent peer culture in contemporary America demeans academic success and scorns students who try to do well in school. Schools are fighting a losing battle against a peer culture that disparages academic success.

- Fewer than one in five students say their friends think it is important to get good grades in school. Less than one-fourth of all students regularly discuss their schoolwork with their friends.

- When asked what crowd in school they would most like to be a part of, nearly one-third said the "partyers" and nearly one-sixth said the "druggies." Only one in ten said the "brains."

- Nearly 20 percent of all students say they do not try as hard as they can in school because they are worried about what their friends might think.

Perhaps most serious, American parents are just as disengaged from schooling as their children are.

- More than half of all students say they could bring home grades of C or worse without their parents getting upset. One-quarter say they could bring home grades of D or worse without upsetting their parents.

- Nearly one-third of students say their parents have no idea how they are doing in school. About one-sixth of all students report that their parents don't care whether they earn good grades in school or not.

• Only about one-fifth of parents consistently attend school programs. More than 40 percent *never* do.

WHY THIS STUDY IS IMPORTANT

The popular press is filled with reports on student achievement—so many, I suspect, that many readers may reasonably ask why the findings presented here merit their attention. It's only fair that I respond to this question before we go any further.

Ours was the first large-scale, systematic study to examine influences on student commitment and performance among youngsters from all walks of life. While most research to date has focused on White, suburban, middle-class children, ours involved a sample of students that truly reflects the diversity that exists within American schools. Whereas most studies of student achievement focus on what takes place within school walls, ours focuses mainly on students' lives outside of school. And while most research on student achievement provides a snapshot of American youth derived from a single survey, ours is based on a three-year study involving not only surveys, but interviews and focus groups as well.

Let me elaborate a bit on why each of these features makes this study important.

A LARGE AND ETHNICALLY DIVERSE SAMPLE

One very important way in which our study differed from previous ones was in the sample of students surveyed. Rather than focusing on a small group of students from one school, or, at the other extreme, on a random sample of American youth, with only a few students drawn from each of many schools around the country, we studied a large sample of students from a limited number of schools that we specifically selected to provide windows to the different sorts of contexts in which today's adolescents come of age. We worked intensively in nine schools in two states—Wisconsin and California—that allowed us to capture the diversity of communities that American students come from and that provide very different pictures of American achievement. Wisconsin typically ranks near the top of the list in statewide comparisons of student achievement. California, in contrast, typically falls in the bottom half of the distribution.

The schools whose students we studied reflect the diversity of educational settings that currently exists in this country. Our research was conducted in a number of middle-class suburban schools serving predominantly White communities; a multiethnic central-city school serving mostly African-American youth; several schools with large numbers of recently arrived Latino and Asian youngsters; a suburban school where Black and White students were integrated through busing; and a rural school serving just several hundred students, many from farm families. Each year, we collected information from over 10,000 students; over the course of the three years of data collection, more than 20,000 different students participated in the research.

Consistent with the changed and changing composition of America's youth population, nearly 40 percent of the students in our study came from ethnic minority families (this 40 percent was nearly evenly split among African-Americans, Asian-Americans, and Hispanic-Americans). More than one-third of the students were living in homes that had been touched by divorce, remarriage, or single parenthood—again, consistent with national data. The socioeconomic status of our students' families varied as well, ranging from lower-class families where parents had not completed high school to professional families in which parents had considerable postgraduate training. As is the case nationally, the vast majority of the students in our sample were from families with a mother who was employed outside the home.

The diversity of our sample was important for a number of reasons. Obviously, having a sample of students from a wide range of ethnic and social backgrounds permits us to have more confidence in the broader generalizability of the findings than would be the case if we studied just one ethnic group, one social class, or one sort of household. But, in combination with the sheer size of the sample, the diversity we had in our study also permitted us to ask many questions that social scientists had not been able to examine previously. For example, because we had large numbers of adolescents from both divorced and nondivorced homes, we were able to do much more than simply compare these two groups of youngsters and ask which group was doing better in school. We were able to look *within* each group (i.e., divorced versus nondivorced families) and ask what it was that differentiated successful students from unsuccessful ones. This enabled us to ask whether the things that "worked" in one group were the same as the things that "worked" in the other. This is a critically important issue, because the advice social scientists give typically comes from studies of only White, middle-class, nondivorced families. Instead of just assuming that this advice is good for students and parents of other backgrounds, we were able to look at this question scientifically.

It is important to emphasize that the schools we studied were average schools—the sort of schools that most children in this country attend. We deliberately avoided studying either private schools or the most impoverished rural or inner-city schools. As to the first of these exclusions, it seemed to us that conclusions based on studies of private schools would be difficult to generalize to the vast majority of school districts in this country. Consequently, had we focused on private schools, our research would be far less informative to the national debate over what to do about our achievement problem and less useful to the vast majority of parents whose children are, and will continue to be, enrolled in public schools. Nevertheless, many of the findings of our research on out-of-school influences on achievement are likely to apply as well to students attending private schools as they do to students in public schools.

As to the exclusion of schools in exceedingly disadvantaged communities from the sample, we felt that the problems associated with the most severe poverty, whether urban or rural, are so devastating and multifaceted that it is simply impossible to consider schools in these communities alongside their counterparts in more advantaged neighborhoods. Understanding the problem of low achievement is difficult enough; trying to understand it in the context of environmental deprivation, crime, teen pregnancy, malnutrition, poor housing, violence, and parental unemployment is a different matter altogether. To be sure, we need to continue to ask how we can better educate youngsters who grow up in communities with chronic economic adversity, and many of the lessons from the present study have important implications for understanding achievement among those adolescents. But being interested in studying school achievement amid abject poverty should not preclude us from also asking how we can raise the achievement of the vast majority of American students, who do not live below the poverty line. If we are to solve America's achievement problem, average students need our attention as well. Indeed, some might even argue that it is both the declining achievement of average students, as well as the poor achievement of disadvantaged students, that forms our country's urgent educational problem.

STUDENTS' HOME LIVES

A second factor that separates our study from previous research on American high school student achievement is the richness of the information we collected. Many educational surveys of young people have large samples, as ours does, but most surveys of this magnitude generally collect only superficial data. The information gathered in such surveys on the family, for example—the most well-studied of the potential out-of-school influences on school performance—is often limited to questions about parents' educational attainment, their occupations, their income, or their marital status. While these factors have proven important predictors of school success—not surprisingly, students do better in school when their parents are wealthier, more educated, employed in more prestigious jobs, and married—research on these variables tells us little about what parents *do* that really makes a difference. Most parents can't change their educational histories, occupations, or household income in any marked ways, and few would change their marital status simply to raise their child's school performance. If parents want to know how they can help their child succeed in school on a daily basis, they need different sorts of information than that provided by studies of family background and student achievement. We collected intensive information from each student on how his or her parents behave, both with regard to school specifically and as parents in general.

Many concrete lessons emerged from the family portion of our study that we think will be invaluable to those interested in knowing how parents can help their child do better in school. As you will read in a later chapter, the good news is that there are a number of practices that parents can engage in that really work—practices that have a discernible payoff in improved grades, more positive attitudes, and a higher level of engagement in school. The bad news, though, is that relatively few parents are doing these things consistently. One goal of this book is to help readers see just how important parents are to their child's academic success and to help parents understand what works—and what doesn't. In so doing, perhaps we can increase the prevalence of effective parenting.

STUDENTS' LIVES OUTSIDE THE HOME

We also spent considerable effort looking at out-of-school settings other than the family. Just as there has been an awful lot of "school-bashing" in discussions of America's achievement problem, there has been a great deal of "parent-bashing" in this debate as well. Our view is that there is much more to the problem than the alleged "decline" of the American family. Accordingly, although we wanted to know how parents were affecting their children's school performance, we also knew that adolescents spend a large amount of their time out of school with their friends, in extracurricular activities, and in after-school jobs. We wondered how these forces in students' lives influenced achievement in combination with the impact of the family. So, in addition to looking at the family's role in achievement, we also studied the contribution of peers, extracurricular activities, and part-time employment.

Our insistence on describing students' home environments in detail extended to our assessment of their time in other settings as well. In studying students' peer relations, for example, we asked questions about their close friends, including a series of questions about who those close friends *are*, so that we were able to compare each adolescent's answers with those of his or her friends to see how they potentially influence each other. This is an important improvement over simply asking adolescents to tell us *about* their friends, since teenagers tend to overstate their similarity to their peers. In addition, we spent considerable time constructing social "maps" of each school and locating each adolescent within the school's peer-group terrain. By the time we had completed this portion of the research, we knew, for instance, which students were "jocks," which were "populars," which were "brains," and which were "druggies." As it turns out, knowing where an individual adolescent fits into the peer culture of his or her school tells us a great deal about that student's orientation toward academics.

The lessons we learned from studying adolescents' time with their friends will be humbling to those who believe that parents, and parents alone, shape their child's school performance. Indeed, in many respects, we found that peers were far more influential than parents in influencing teenagers' achievement, especially when it comes to day-to-day matters such as doing homework, concentrating in class, or taking their studies seriously. In some cases, the influence of peers actually overwhelmed that of parents, undoing whatever influence parents tried to exert at home. But the influence of friends was not always for the worse—while we did uncover many instances of "bad" friends countering the best intentions of "good" parents, we also found plenty of evidence for the power of "good" friends to compensate for deficiencies in the home environment. This information enabled us to carefully examine the role of peers in adolescent achievement—as well as how parents can be more effective in light of the power of the peer group.

Today's adolescents spend considerable time outside of school in structured settings, on jobs and in school-sponsored extracurricular activities. For example, one important, and often overlooked, part of the achievement problem is the tremendous amount of time American students spend working in part-time jobs—in restaurants, supermarkets, and retail stores. Given the extraordinary time commitment that so many students make to after-school employment—about two-thirds of high school students work at some time during the school year, and half of all working students work in excess of fifteen hours weekly—we were interested in knowing how having an extensive obligation to an after-school activity affected students' engagement and commitment to school itself. Does holding down a part-time job make students more responsible and better organized, or do the demands of after-school employment interfere with school? This question is especially important, because after-school work for high school students is quite uncommon in other countries, and because student employment is one facet of adolescent life that adults actually have some control over, through child labor laws, regulations regarding work permits, and parental permission to work.

In keeping with our intention to study school within the context of students' whole lives—rather than looking just at school itself—we also asked many questions about other aspects of students' psychological functioning. As a result, the students completed dozens of standardized measures of psychological adjustment, including those measuring their self-conceptions, motivation, and sense of responsibility. Given the current concern about problematic aspects of adolescence in this country, we also collected extensive information on various indicators of *maladjustment*: involvement in delinquent activities, drug and alcohol use, and symptoms of psychological distress.

FOLLOWING STUDENTS OVER TIME

An additional strength of our study is that we followed students over time—some for as many as three years. Each year, for three consecutive years, we surveyed all of the students who were enrolled in our participating schools. During the second year, therefore, many of the students who had participated in the first year were in our study once again. (We did not try to track down students who had graduated, dropped out of school, or moved out of the district.) In fact, many of the students who were freshmen or sophomores at the beginning of the study were surveyed repeatedly over three years, until they were juniors or seniors.

This longitudinal design permitted us to investigate how different influences on student achievement unfold over the course of high school and helped us get a bit closer to disentangling cause and effect. Finding that certain parenting practices go hand in hand with better school performance is informative, but it is entirely possible that the better school performance influenced the parenting practices, rather than the reverse. We might find, for example, that students do better in school when their parents are more involved in education, but without longitudinal information, we could not be sure that the involvement actually led to the better performance. Indeed, it is perfectly plausible that the parents of high-achieving students became more involved as a result of their child's school success. Having data that span three years allowed us to see whether the factors that we think enhance student achievement really do occur before, and not just alongside, the improved school performance.

HOW WE GOT OUR INFORMATION

Our primary means of collecting data was through questionnaires administered to students in their classrooms. Students were surveyed for two class periods each year; each questionnaire was between ten and sixteen pages long, and each contained several hundred individual items. Members of our research staff were present at the school to help administer the surveys and answer students' questions. Whenever possible, we employed widely used questions that have proved valid and reliable in studies of high school youth, rather than inventing our own means of assessment.

The questionnaires were anonymous and confidential. Instead of having students put their names on their surveys, we used identification numbers in a way that protected the student's anonymity while permitting us to match each student's questionnaire with the others that he or she completed over the course of the study. When an entire classroom was finished filling out their surveys, a member of our research staff collected the students' questionnaires and sealed them in an envelope, so that no one other than our research team could have access to students' responses. Students were assured that their individual answers would not be seen by teachers, administrators, parents, or other students.

FOCUS GROUPS AND PERSONAL INTERVIEWS

Surveys permit a researcher to cast a wide net over a large array of variables and collect data on a large sample. But there is much that cannot be learned from paper-and-pencil surveys, especially on subjects that are not easily captured on paper-and-pencil instruments. We therefore included other methods of collecting information.

In order to get a better picture of the peer crowds in each school, we conducted a series of focus groups with students from different ethnic groups and different grade levels. These focus groups helped us identify the major crowds within each school and the adolescents who were perceived by other students as the crowd leaders. We then asked small samples of students in each school to "locate" their classmates within the crowd structure of their school. We did this by presenting students with a list of names (and sometimes photographs) and having them tell us which students were "jocks," which were "brains," which were "druggies," and so forth. In part of the questionnaire, we also asked students to characterize themselves as a member of one of the crowds.

Finally, we conducted intensive one-on-one interviews with six hundred teenagers who were selected on the basis of their ethnicity and school performance (we deliberately selected equal numbers of high-, medium-, and low-achieving students from each ethnic group). In these interviews, we asked a series of questions about the student's school-related behavior, attitudes, and values. As well, we conducted separate interviews with more than five hundred sets of parents, again with an emphasis on their child's schooling and on their roles as parents.

All in all, the students in our study provided extensive information on their family life, their friends, their experiences in the classroom, and their time out of school on playing fields and behind the counters of fast-food restaurants. They answered hundreds of questions about their study habits, their course work, their educational aspirations, and their attitudes and values. We wanted to know not only how well they were doing, but how hard they were working, how they viewed their own successes and failures in school, and how they made sense of school in light of the influences they encountered at home, with their friends, and in other out-of-school settings.

Together, these different sources of information provided an illuminating look at the daily lives of American adolescents and their families, and of the impact that events outside of the classroom have on students' engagement and performance in school.

THE REAL PROBLEM

One of the extraordinary changes that has taken place in American schools in the past twenty-five years is the shift in the relative proportions of engaged and disengaged students. Teachers have always encountered students who were difficult to interest and hard to motivate, but the number of these students was considerably smaller in the past than it is today. Two decades ago, a teacher in an average high school in this country could expect to have three or four "difficult" students in a class of thirty. Today, teachers in these same schools are expected to teach to classrooms in which nearly half of the students have "checked out."

The widespread disengagement of America's students is a problem with enormous implications and profound potential consequences. Although it is less visible, less dramatic, and less commented upon than other social problems involving youth—crime, pregnancy, violence—student disengagement is more pervasive and in some ways potentially more harmful to the future well-being of American society.

TWO

A Nation at Risk, A Nation in Denial

If we have become dangerously accustomed to the image of American students as disengaged from school, we have also become dangerously inured to stories about their abysmal level of academic accomplishment. News stories about the low level of achievement among American teenagers have become so commonplace that they now seem almost clichéd. Almost on a daily basis, we hear about the dismal performance of our students in international competitions, about the declining skills of new entrants to the workforce, and about the lack of preparation that high school graduates bring to their college classes. Even the most positive commentators on education have to admit that levels of student achievement in this country have either declined or remained stagnant in recent decades.

A NATION AT RISK

These disheartening data were summarized by education expert Diane Ravitch, in her 1995 book *National Standards in American Education*. Ravitch, now on the faculty at New York University, had previously served as assistant secretary of educational research and improvement at the U.S. Department of Education. She is widely admired, by liberals and conservatives alike, as one of our country's preeminent educational historians and as a rational and temperate commentator on the state of schooling in America.

In her book, Ravitch draws on data from diverse sources to illustrate the claim that achievement in the United States is in a very sorry state. Because her summary of this evidence is so thorough and so recent, there is no reason to repeat it here. Instead, let me simply restate the main conclusions of her analyses—conclusions that have been reached by other investigators as well.

SAT SCORES HAVE DECLINED SIGNIFICANTLY SINCE THE MID-1960S

Scores on the Scholastic Aptitude Test (SAT), a standardized exam taken by millions of high school juniors and seniors seeking college admission, have fallen considerably since the mid-1960s. Although the decline did reverse itself somewhat during the early 1980s, SAT scores have never returned to their pre-1975 levels. Furthermore, scores have begun to fall again during the past two years. Simply put, students taking the SAT today are not performing as well as their counterparts did twenty-five or thirty years ago.

The drop in SAT scores first came to the public's attention in 1975. Initially, critics of the research on the SAT decline raised concerns about the interpretation of the data, arguing that the apparent drop in performance was due to an increase in the diversity of the population of students taking the test. As more and more high school students have sought admission to college, the argument went, the number of students taking the SAT has grown, and most of this growth has occurred among lower-scoring students. Presumably, the most able students in our high schools have been taking the SAT all along, and the additional test-takers in more recent years have come from the less able youngsters who in the past would not have applied to college. Any drop in average SAT scores over time might not reflect a genuine decline in student achievement, but simply a dragging down of the average by the addition of less able students to the population of test-takers.

This interpretation—that the SAT drop wasn't real, but was due merely to changes in who was taking the test—placed a curious bit of self-congratulatory spin on what otherwise might have been seen as a worrisome trend.

The decline in SAT scores wasn't a problem, some commentators noted—it simply showed that our educational system was becoming more open and democratic, and that access to higher education was expanding. (This was the politically correct way of saying that more non-White students were taking the SAT and that these students were bringing down the national average.) The idea that the SAT decline was nothing to worry about—and, indeed, that it might even be *good* news—was the prevailing view during most of the 1980s.

Several detailed analyses of changes in SAT scores conducted during the past several years reveal that only a small part of the observed decline was attributable to changes in the test-taking population, however. Two lines of evidence in particular call this interpretation into question. First, as Ravitch points out, the decline in SAT scores continued to occur even during years in which the number of high school students taking the test did not increase appreciably. In fact, scores fell most rapidly during the 1970s, when the size and composition of the test-taking population changed hardly at all.

Second, the contention that the SAT drop was due mainly to the increase in the number of non-White test-takers is simply untrue. When White students' test scores are examined separately, one finds that the decline in performance within this subgroup is identical to the overall drop—suggesting that the larger pattern of decline was due neither to the democratization of the test nor to the expansion of educational opportunities to ethnic minorities. According to one careful analysis, in fact, the SAT drop cannot be explained by changes in the racial, socioeconomic, or gender composition of the test-taking population. Contrary to the oddly reassuring (and transparently self-serving) account that White, middle-class social scientists promoted, the decline in SAT scores that took place after the mid-1960s was just as prevalent among White, middle-class children as it was among less affluent and minority youngsters.

THE DECLINE IN STUDENT PERFORMANCE IS NOT LIMITED TO SAT SCORES

Some critics may rightly contend that the SAT is not a perfect measure of academic achievement. But the disturbing pattern seen in the steady decline in SAT scores is not limited to this one index of scholastic accomplishment;

it is seen in other measures of achievement as well. A similarly discouraging picture emerges if we look, for example, at the results of a federally administered assessment called the National Assessment of Educational Progress (NAEP), or, as it is more colloquially known, "The Nation's Report Card."

The NAEP regularly tests student proficiency in four areas: mathematics, science, reading, and writing. The value of the NAEP assessment is that the test and its scoring have remained unchanged for many years. Moreover, the scoring of the NAEP relies less on an assessment of the "facts" students know, and more on an assessment of more general skills. (Since the importance of some of these facts may change over time, students from different eras will be exposed to them in varying degrees in school. Changes in scores on fact-based tests are therefore open to a variety of interpretations, among them, that fluctuations in scores simply reflect fluctuations in the emphases that schools place on certain bodies of information.) Thus, for example, the NAEP assessment of writing emphasizes students' ability to produce a coherent and persuasive written argument, rather than their knowledge of specific rules of grammar; the assessment of science proficiency assesses students' ability to apply scientific knowledge to the solution of a problem, rather than their possession of that knowledge alone, and so forth. Overall, then, the annual NAEP assessment provides a reasonably good barometer of how the nation's students are faring.

How well are our nation's high school students doing today? In science, they score higher than they did during the early 1980s, but not as high as their counterparts scored in 1970. In math, they score higher than they did in the early 1980s, but no higher than they did in the early 1970s. (Math data were not available for years prior to 1973, but given the NAEP science trends and the SAT mathematics data, it is almost certain that math proficiency is lower today than it was prior to 1973.) In reading, NAEP scores today are slightly higher than they were in 1971, but there has been no improvement in reading scores since 1984. And in writing, which was not assessed prior to 1984, there has been no change in proficiency whatsoever since that time. Moreover, given the pre-1970 SAT verbal test scores, there is good reason to think that students' writing proficiency is significantly lower today than it was in 1970. If you are doubtful, just ask anyone who has been teaching at an American university for the past twenty-five years.

POOR ACADEMIC PERFORMANCE IS APPARENT EVEN
AMONG OUR TOP STUDENTS

Just as the SAT drop cannot be attributed to a dramatic influx of low-scoring students into the test-taking pool, neither can the NAEP data be dismissed as indicative of problems only among our least able students. Because the NAEP is administered to all students, regardless of their post-high-school plans, the composition of the population tested does not fluctuate from year to year as much as the SAT test-taking population might. More important, though, the percentage of students performing at the top levels on the national assessments is shockingly low, especially considering that the definition of excellence on these tests is exceedingly liberal.

To earn a top score on the mathematics portion of the NAEP, for example, a high school junior need not demonstrate any skills beyond algebra. Yet, in 1992, as in 1978, only 7 percent of high school juniors scored in this category. The news on science is no more encouraging: in 1992, only one in ten juniors could "infer relationships and draw conclusions using detailed scientific knowledge," the criterion for scoring at the highest proficiency level in that domain. Thus, even if NAEP scores in math and science have risen since the 1980s, in absolute terms we have very little to be positive about. As two social scientists noted, even if today's high school students are no worse educated than their counterparts were in the early 1980s, "this does not mean that they are well educated by absolute standards, nor that they are well-educated enough to meet the challenges from ever-stronger competitors overseas."

The situation is not better in the humanities; actually, it is worse. The 1994 NAEP report called the gains in seventeen-year-olds' reading proficiency since 1971 "encouraging," a kind overstatement, to say the least. Indeed, when one looks closely at the report, it is difficult to find the source of encouragement. Average scores on this subtest have risen less than 2 percent over the past two decades. Moreover, only 7 percent of seventeen-year-olds are able to "synthesize and learn from specialized reading materials," the generous criterion that places a student at the top level on this test. Fewer than 2 percent of juniors earned top marks on the writing assessment, where the highest proficiency level was characterized simply by "coherent" writing that *"tended* to contain supportive details and discussion that contributed to the effectiveness of the response" (my italics). Evidently, this is now all it takes to be judged an excellent writer by American educational standards.

POOR ACHIEVEMENT IS CHARACTERISTIC OF STUDENTS AT ALL GRADE LEVELS

Analyses of the NAEP data also show that America's achievement problem is not limited to today's high school students—the cohort born in the late 1970s and early 1980s. One might have hoped that the bad news about American achievement would have been limited to a specific age group, and that whatever changes we have made in our schools since the early 1980s have borne fruit. Not so, however: NAEP results for nine- and thirteen-year-olds are just as discouraging as they are for seventeen-year-olds. With one small exception—an upturn in thirteen-year-olds' writing scores between 1990 and 1992 that was so inconsistent with other data that even the authors of the 1994 NAEP report (who, as we have seen, are prone to putting an optimistic spin on the assessment's findings) cautioned against overinterpretation. There have been no gains in writing proficiency in the past decade among nine-year-olds, and no gains to speak of in reading, math, or science proficiency among either nine- or thirteen-year-olds since the early 1970s. At the elementary and middle school levels, American student achievement is as uniformly low and stagnant as it is at the high school level.

POOR ACHIEVEMENT IS CHARACTERISTIC OF STUDENTS IN ALL SOCIAL CLASSES

As I previously mentioned, when the SAT decline was first announced in 1975, commentators were quick to point the finger at poor and minority test-takers for bringing the national average down, an account that deflected attention away from the fact that SAT scores had dropped in other socioeconomic and ethnic groups as well. Even today, the media attention given to the educational difficulties of youngsters growing up in the nation's poorest communities has focused our discussion of achievement in America around the special problems of inner-city children and urban schools. And while it is of course true that the achievement problems of poor, urban, minority youth are substantial, the results of research involving affluent, suburban, White youngsters provide little cause for celebration.

Because the 1994 NAEP report presented trends in achievement scores broken down by type of community, it is possible to look separately at the performance of students who are enrolled in what are characterized by the authors of the report as "advantaged urban schools"—schools in metropolitan areas and their surrounding suburbs "where a high proportion of the students' parents are in professional or managerial positions." Based on these data analyses, there is little reason for middle-class parents to be cheerful about their children's educational performance—nor is there any reason to lull ourselves into thinking that America's educational problems are limited to poor, minority youngsters attending inner-city schools.

Among seventeen-year-olds enrolled in advantaged urban and suburban schools, the only area in which average proficiency has changed over time has been writing, and in this case, the data indicate that the writing proficiency of these students actually has *declined* over time. Scores in math, science, and reading—low to begin with—have not changed at all. Among thirteen-year-olds from comparably advantaged schools, the same picture emerges: no improvement in math, science, or reading proficiency, and a decline in writing skills. The only good news comes from the data on nine-year-olds from advantaged urban schools, whose average science and math scores have improved over the past decade, albeit very slightly. But this improvement is not due to an increase in the percentage of students earning top marks on the NAEP. Even among students attending affluent urban and suburban schools, at no age level, in no subject area, has there been an increase in the past decade in the proportion of students who score at the highest level of proficiency.

AMERICAN STUDENTS FARE POORLY
IN INTERNATIONAL COMPARISONS

The problem of low and stagnating achievement in this country is also revealed in international comparisons of student test scores. As has been widely publicized, American students fare worse than their peers from virtually all other industrialized nations, across virtually all subject areas, and especially in mathematics and science. Numerous international comparisons have been made during the past fifteen years, and on virtually all of them American students score at or below the median of the participating countries. Moreover, the gap between our students' achievement and that of students in other countries is not only large; it is growing wider with each passing year.

The poor showing of American students relative to those from other countries was highlighted in the oft-cited 1983 report on the sorry state of American education, *A Nation at Risk*. Yet, in the same way that some commentators attempted to dismiss the SAT decline as a statistical artifact that was due to changes in the composition of the test-taking pool, others attempted to write off the international comparisons on similar grounds. Specifically, it was suggested that international achievement contrasts are inherently unfair, because the United States enrolls a more heterogeneous population of students in our secondary schools than do other countries. Unlike the United States, most other industrialized countries separate students into different schools on the basis of ability tests administered prior to high school. Comparisons of groups of American students that include both college-bound and non-college-bound adolescents with international samples that are restricted to students in exclusively college-preparatory schools will necessarily make American students look bad. Critics of the international comparisons noted that it was important to consider these differences before drawing conclusions about America's relative standing on the international achievement ladder.

There are two main ways to address the issue of comparability in international test comparisons. One is to make the international assessments early enough in children's education, while they are still grouped heterogeneously in other countries, as they are here. In perhaps the most well-designed and comprehensive cross-national study of achievement to do this, by Harold Stevenson and his colleagues at the University of Michigan, American youngsters were found to lag well behind their peers from Taiwan, Japan, or China—with deficiencies evident as early as kindergarten and apparent throughout elementary school. And, contrary to popular stereotypes, the achievement gap between American and Asian youngsters was not only in mathematics. As the researchers noted:

A close examination of American children's academic achievement rapidly dispels any notion that we face a problem of limited scope. The problem is not restricted to a certain age level or to a particular academic subject. Whether we look at the average scores for schools or at the scores for individuals, we find evidence of serious and pervasive weakness.

Another way of making the international contrast more comparable is to limit it to a comparison of only the top students here and abroad—that is, to compare our best students with the best from other countries. Several international comparisons have done just this, by including only those American students who have been enrolled in our schools' most challenging and advanced classes. Sadly, America fares no better when we approach the problem from this angle: Comparisons of even our *best* students with those from other nations are discouraging. Indeed, in mathematics and science, our top students know less than students in other industrialized countries who are considered merely average by their countries' standards.

As was the case with the early criticism of the SAT studies, the argument that conclusions drawn from international comparisons are inherently flawed has not stood up to careful scrutiny. As a recent analysis by the National Center for Education Statistics (the official number-crunching division of the U.S. Department of Education) concluded:

> [T]here is one consistent message. Students from the United States, regardless of grade level, generally lag behind many of their counterparts from other developed countries in both mathematics and science achievement. . . . Generally, the "best students" in the United States do less well on the international surveys when compared with the "best students" from other countries.

THE COSTS OF AMERICAN UNDERACHIEVEMENT

It was really not until the achievement problem was put into an economic context that the American public and politicians began to give it some serious attention. Beginning with the 1983 publication of *A Nation at Risk*, and continuing well into the 1990s, much was written about the potential adverse impact of the achievement decline on America's ability to compete in the international economy. The arguments have been straightforward enough, and few experts have questioned them: as our country's economic success comes to depend more and more on the presence of highly skilled employees, our competitiveness will be increasingly linked to our ability to produce a highly educated labor force.

Most economists predict that the poor record of academic achievement demonstrated by our students relative to their counterparts in other countries will have devastating effects on the American economy if the trend is not reversed. As the authors of *A Nation at Risk* put it, in 1983, "If an unfriendly foreign power had attempted to impose on America the mediocre educational performance that exists today, we might well have viewed it as an act of war. As it stands, we have allowed this to happen to ourselves. . . . We have, in effect, been committing an act of unthinking, unilateral educational disarmament."

The situation is no better today—and in many respects it is worse—than when this urgent statement was issued, because the gap between American educational achievement and achievement in other countries has widened since 1983. Analysts agree today that America will not be able to compete successfully in the international marketplace without substantially increasing the skill level and knowledge of its labor force. What they disagree on, as we shall see, is how best to accomplish this.

To date, we have only begun to feel the impact of our achievement problem in the economic marketplace. But we can already see quite clearly the devastating effects of low and stagnating elementary and high school achievement on American colleges and universities. Today, three-fourths of American college faculty report that the entering students they teach lack basic skills. At one of the local community colleges in Philadelphia, it has been reported that the average reading level of incoming freshmen is between third and sixth grade. Current estimates are that between 30 and 40 percent of entering freshmen *across the country* require remedial coursework in reading and writing, and an even higher number in mathematics, in order to pursue "college-level" coursework. And those of us who teach at the university level know full well that the definition of "college-level" has been sliding down a slippery slope for a good many years.

What has this meant for American institutions of higher education? One consequence has been the diversion of resources in already tight university budgets away from precisely the sort of high-level educational preparation on which our country's economic survival depends. In the course of researching this chapter, my research assistants and I attempted to gather information from several national data centers, including the National Center for Education Statistics (NCES), on the annual expenditure by American colleges and universities on remedial education and related services. Interestingly, no one could provide us with even an approximate estimate of how much we are spending (curious, indeed, in a nation for whom statistics-gathering is a way of life). Part of the problem, one of our colleagues at NCES explained, is that colleges and universities often do not label remedial courses as such, because they want to hide the fact that so much of their students' degree credits are granted for pre-college-level work.

As a consequence of this sort of record-keeping legerdemain, it is virtually impossible to know what proportion of university instructional expenditures are devoted to remedial versus regular instruction. It is safe to say, however, that, if between one-third and one-half of the entering college students in this country require remedial education, the declining achievement of American youth must be costing our colleges and universities a large fortune. Remedial courses must be staffed, which takes instructors out of regular classes, leading to fewer offerings, more crowded classes, or the need to hire additional faculty to teach regular courses. Student-faculty ratios need to be lower in remedial courses than in regular ones, which makes remedial instruction more expensive to provide. Physical space, which is always at a premium on college campuses, must be allocated for reading, writing, and math "laboratories" (a euphemism if there ever was one), leaving less space for regular instruction and research facilities, and often necessitating the construction of new facilities or the renovation of old ones. Not included in these costs is the added money that universities must spend each year on student retention for undergraduates who take remedial coursework—on special social and academic programs designed to prevent students from dropping out—because universities know that students who enter college unprepared are more apt to leave school before graduating.

The cost of having poorly prepared students attend our colleges and universities is also apparent when we look at its impact on the regular curriculum. Let me use an example from the department in which I teach, at Temple University. Most university psychology departments require undergraduate majors to take a semester of coursework on psychological statistics. When I first arrived at Temple, I was surprised (and pleased) to discover that our psychology majors were required to take not one semester of statistics, but two. It was only after I commented favorably on this requirement to a colleague that I learned that the department had been forced to split what had been a one-semester course into a full-year one, because so many students needed two semesters to master what their previous counterparts had been able to learn in one. Of course, along the way what was one four-credit course became two four-credit courses, and anyone looking at students' transcripts (like myself) would be easily fooled into thinking that the students had double the statistics preparation that they had actually received. And consider the economics of this practice: in terms of faculty time, it now costs our department twice as much to teach the same course; consequently, we must either raise faculty teaching loads, hire additional instructors, or eliminate a more advanced course from the department's offerings. When you consider that this sort of practice has become standard fare at colleges and universities across the country, in all academic disciplines, you begin to see the magnitude and depth of the problem.

Most discussions of the economic costs of the achievement decline focus on the long-term implications for the American economy. But there are immediate costs to American business, which must make do with a labor supply that is inadequately educated and poorly trained. A recent report from the National Adult Literacy Study provides telling evidence of how poorly equipped our college graduates are to function in a highly competitive international economy in which success depends on a highly skilled, literate labor force. The study found that fewer than half of all American college graduates—not half of all Americans, but half of all *college graduates*—were able to write a coherent essay describing an argument presented in a newspaper article they read, or could contrast the opinions expressed in two opposing editorials. Only one-third of the college graduates could write a brief letter explaining a billing error. Only 11 percent of four-year-college graduates, and only 4 percent of two-year-college graduates, were sufficiently literate to be able to summarize, based on information they were given, two

ways that attorneys may challenge prospective jurors. Evidently, even the remedial education on which colleges are spending so much money is failing.
Moreover, if American colleges and universities are devoting proportionately
more of their resources to remedial education, they are devoting less to advanced instruction, which means that even literate college graduates today
probably have had less exposure to challenging course work than their counterparts did in previous eras.

If more than one-third of all college entrants require remedial education, imagine the academic deficiencies of the high school graduates who do
not go on to college or, worse still, the young adults who do not even complete high school. The costs to industry of training these individuals in skills
they should have acquired in school are enormous. And, of course, the costs
of not training them—in lost business, diminished productivity, added supervision costs, and errors on the job—are absolutely staggering. The next
time you find yourself being served by a twenty-five-year-old cashier who is
incapable of making change without relying on an electronic cash register,
try to imagine what it must be like to have to manage a storeful of such employees.

A NATION IN DENIAL

The evidence that there is a serious achievement problem in this country—
a problem that has been with us for close to twenty-five years now—seems
incontrovertible. Yet the American public has reacted to stories about our
failing students with a curious mixture of denial, anger, and boredom (ironically, the same mix of emotions characteristic of the alienated students we
so often see on television). Tired of having our children "bashed," and irri-
tated at the constant criticism of our schools and our culture, otherwise
thoughtful columnists and contributors to the nation's op-ed pages routinely react to reports about the poor showing of America's students on standardized tests by criticizing the tests, the researchers, the science behind the
studies, or the fact that the question is even being examined. Harold Stevenson and James Stigler, whose cross-cultural research on achievement is ar-
guably the best and most careful work in the area, commented on this
curiosity in their book *The Learning Gap*:

Despite articles in the press and reports in other media, Americans persist in believing that nothing is seriously wrong—that there is no crisis. . . . [Journalists] express . . . disdain for comparative studies: "Well, here we go again," [wrote columnist Jeff Greenfield]. "Once more, for the 3,207th time an Officially Important Survey has revealed that our children are a bunch of morons. This time, the Officially Important Survey reveals, they have been proven a bunch of mathematical morons. And you know what? I don't think I care all that much."

Similarly, surveys of parents consistently show that while we recognize that something is wrong with our educational system, we are likely to believe that our own children's schools are doing a fine job—a sort of "not my kid's school" reaction. When parents are asked to "grade" their child's school, they award A's and B's; when asked to evaluate the nation's schools in general, they give much lower grades.

Our capacity to deny the existence of a genuine achievement problem in this country in the face of overwhelming and consistent evidence to the contrary is unwavering, although the denial has taken different forms in different eras. In the 1970s, when the SAT decline was first announced, we were quick to deny the problem by attributing it to changes in the composition of the test-taking group. In the 1980s, when the results of a major international achievement comparison were highlighted in *A Nation at Risk*—a comparison involving nineteen academic tests on which United States youngsters never placed first and were last seven times—we denied the problem by claiming that international comparisons were inherently biased against us. As I've noted, neither of these arguments has held up under careful analysis. Both the SAT decline and the poor showing of American youngsters in international comparisons are genuine.

In 1994, the distance we were willing to go in order to deny that there is a significant achievement problem in this country reached new heights (or perhaps, new depths). The Educational Testing Service (ETS) announced in 1994 that it was establishing new norms for the Scholastic Aptitude Test to take into account the diminished academic competence of American high school students. As of 1995, the test was to be "recentered," so that in order to earn an average score on the test—a combined score of 1,000—a 1995 high school student would not have to know as much as a student would have known in the past in order to earn the same score. In other words, a score that is labeled "average" on the 1995 SAT test is equivalent, in terms of absolute performance, to a "below-average" SAT score pre-1995. Similarly, a performance that would have been judged just "average" before 1995 is now considered "above average."

To get a sense of just how bizarre this "recentering" is, consider, for example, the following analogy. In 1994, a news story appeared in the national media indicating that, despite the widespread publication during the 1980s of information on healthy patterns of diet and exercise, the average American had become considerably fatter over the past decade. This announcement prompted further discussion about the causes and consequences of obesity, and about public health steps that might reverse the pattern. But imagine if, in response to this story, instead of attempting to understand and reverse the trend, medical experts simply announced that in 1995 they were establishing new, and more generous, weight norms for obesity. Where the obesity cutoff for a medium-frame, five-foot-ten-inch man had been 193 pounds in 1994, the cutoff was going to be "recentered," beginning in 1995, at 215 pounds. A 170-pound, five-foot-five-inch woman who had been obese in 1994, would no longer wear that label in 1995, since the cutoff for obesity was going to start at 190. From a public health perspective, would it be any comfort to know that the same degree of overweight in 1994 was no longer labeled "obese" in 1995? More to the point, would changing the obesity norms do anything other than make individuals *more* accepting of being overweight? By the same token, will the "recentering" of the SAT have any effect other than to make us forget that American achievement has been declining?

ETS tried to put a different spin on the recentering story, rationalizing the modification as necessary due to a change in the composition of the test-taking population. But this, in essence, was nothing more than admitting that the students who are taking the SAT, and applying to college, are not as well prepared today as their counterparts were previously; with the recentering, we just wouldn't be reminded of it so often. And, although ETS promised that students' newly normed scores would be reported alongside information on the old scoring scale (here's your current score; here's what your score would have been had you taken the test before 1994), it is all too likely, given our short collective memory for such matters, that in a few years the old scale will be little more than a distant recollection. The recentering of the SAT will have the effect of further diverting our attention from the problem of diminished achievement.

Despite the ETS announcement that it was "recentering" the SAT—if you really stop and think about it, an astounding admission of how grim things actually have become—the story generated about two days' worth of media attention, and then it slipped quietly away, almost as if it were too embarrassing to discuss in public. Apparently, as evidenced by the flurry of attention given later that same year to the publication of Robert T. Michael's *Sex in America*, which presented the findings from a major national survey on sexual behavior, we feel more comfortable discussing the fact that Johnny's parents don't have sex very often than the fact that Johnny can't read, write, or add.

THE GLORIFICATION OF STUPIDITY

While adults in the worlds of social science, educational measurement, journalism, and politics attempted to deny the achievement decline by manipulating the data, pleading boredom, and engaging in academic discussions about alternative explanations of the findings, the general public was engaged in its own curious form of denial. During the late 1980s and early 1990s a different but no less telling reaction to the achievement decline appeared—what might be called the "glorification of stupidity." Suddenly, it seemed that people of all ages, but adolescents and young adults in particular, were all fascinated with television shows and films in which the lead characters were admired for being insipid, anti-intellectual, or just plain stupid—"The Simpsons," "Married . . . with Children," *Wayne's World*, "Beavis and Butt-head," *Dumb and Dumber*, *Billy Madison*—the list goes on and on. Nor was the admiration of idiots limited to young audiences: *Forrest Gump*, the 1994 film that mistook stupidity for folksy common sense, was both a box-office smash among adults and the winner of multiple Academy Awards.

I am not suggesting that the glorification of stupidity has in any way caused, or even exacerbated, the achievement decline. But it must be more than coincidental that the widespread popularity of characters whose most salient trait is ignorance occurred at a time when the level of intellectual accomplishment among young people was itself exceedingly low. Although foolish characters have often drawn laughs from young audiences (and from older ones, as well), fools historically have played secondary roles in the shows and films in which they appeared, and they frequently were *clever* fools. Never before have so many lead characters been defined by their lack of knowledge, their disdain for education, and their limited intellectual abilities. And never before have characters like this served as *role models* for so many young people.

Why should today's adolescents and young adults be so drawn to a group of anti-intellectual morons? One reason, I think, is that the glorification of stupidity in the popular culture provides some strange sort of comfort for those who are genuinely ignorant in real life. When Bart, Beavis, or Billy expresses his disdain for learning, shows off his lack of understanding of even the most simple concepts, or grinningly shrugs off a failing grade in school, stupidity seems not quite so awful—perhaps even a bit endearing. And, of course, ill-educated audiences can take solace in the knowledge that no matter how ignorant they themselves may be, they are at least one step ahead of the morons at whom they're laughing.

THE SAD TRUTH

The data on student achievement in America during the past twenty-five years point to an inescapable conclusion: American student achievement today is barely at the level it was in the mid-1970s, and in many respects, student achievement is significantly lower than it was twenty-five years ago. Although we have tried our best to find alternative explanations for the decline, the evidence clearly shows that the achievement drop is genuine, substantial, and pervasive across ethnic, socioeconomic, and age groups. Moreover, there is no indication from recent assessments that this situation is changing, and some indication, as evidenced in recent reports on declining SAT scores, that it is worsening once again. To top it all off, our definition of educational excellence has eroded nearly to the point of meaninglessness, and yet, only a handful of students qualify for the dubious distinction of placing in the top category. As my colleague Dan Koretz, writing for the Congressional Budget Office in 1986 concluded, the existence of an "overall drop in achievement [entailing] sizeable declines in higher-level skills, such as inference and problem-solving, is beyond question."

Despite our attempts at denying that there is a problem—critiquing the achievement studies over technical details, trying to silence the messengers of bad news, dumbing down the curriculum on college campuses so that the achievement decline doesn't look as bad as it really is, changing the way achievement is measured and assessed—the issue will not go away. If we delay facing the truth—that we have an achievement crisis of gargantuan proportions in this country—solving the problem will become only more difficult and more costly.

THREE

School Reform Is Not the Solution

For the past fifteen years, the frighteningly miserable achievement of America's youth has grabbed the attention of our country's highest political leaders, regardless of their leanings. Indeed, in an era in which politicians can agree on precious few goals, improving the educational performance of America's students is one idea that has received resounding bipartisan support. *A Nation at Risk*, the rallying document for the current school reform movement which warned that "the educational foundations of our society are presently being eroded by a rising tide of mediocrity," was produced during the Reagan administration and published in 1983. In 1989, President Bush and the nation's governors held an educational summit meeting that culminated in the drafting of a set of educational goals that were to be met by the end of the twentieth century. Early in his administration, President Clinton announced yet another initiative designed to boost American student achievement by the year 2000. For nearly fifteen years now, under Republicans and Democrats alike, educational policy-makers have been engaged in a never-ending discussion of ways to solve the problem of low student achievement in America.

Despite their different political bases, most of the suggestions for change to emerge from these various presidential commissions and task forces have focused on what has been broadly referred to as "school reform": experiments with school curricula (i.e., *what* students are taught), instructional methods (i.e., *how* students are taught), school schedules (i.e., *when* students are taught), school organization and choice (i.e., *where* students are taught), and teacher selection and training (i.e., *who* does the teaching). In general, liberals have endorsed efforts to pour greater amounts of money into schools in order to increase students' "opportunities to learn," whereas conservatives have championed programs that increase parents' choice of schools and that return schools "back to basics." Despite these differences, however, the focus of the proposed interventions is always some aspect of our educational system.

In response to these suggestions for educational reform, government institutions and private foundations have spent massive amounts of money on research designed to transform America's schools. In one blue-ribbon report after another, the American public has been told that if we change how we organize our schools, change how and what we teach in our classrooms, and change how we select, train, and compensate our teachers, we will see improvements in our children's educational performance. Many such reforms have been tried across the country—some, admittedly, only halfheartedly, but others, both thoughtfully and in good faith. And many of these reform efforts continue today.

What do we have to show for the mounds of money and millions of hours that have been spent on school reform during the past fifteen years? Although there are occasional success stories in the media about a school here or a program there that has turned students' performance around—stories which are widely publicized in the popular media precisely because they are so unusual—the competence of American students overall has not improved. (Not surprisingly, the school reform efforts that fail almost always go unpublicized, so we really do not know just how unusual the successes are.) The proportions of high school juniors scoring in the top categories on the math, science, reading, and writing portions of the NAEP assessment have not changed in any meaningful way in two decades. As I noted in chapter 2, SAT scores have not risen since the early 1980s, and today they remain lower than they were in the early 1970s; indeed, they even dropped somewhat during the late 1980s and early 1990s. And our teenagers are still among the academically worst prepared in the industrialized world. It is safe to say that few aspects of educational reform tried during the past two decades have yielded systematically encouraging results.

Some educational reformers have argued that student achievement as it is assessed on standardized measures, such as the SAT, the NAEP tests, or the achievement-test batteries used in international comparisons, is not the right measure of whether educational reform has succeeded. But, while it is true that there is more to intelligence than scoring well on the SAT or NAEP examinations, it is difficult to imagine an objective alternative to these standardized tests that would yield a markedly different picture of the state of achievement in contemporary America. Moreover, there is obvious value in continuing to track student achievement using measures that have been employed over a long period of time, so as to be able to chart trends historically. Frankly, discussions about finding other ways to evaluate student achievement—no doubt with the hope of finding *some* indication of successful reform, somehow, somewhere—evade, rather than illuminate, the problem.

It is always difficult to know how to interpret a pattern of results that indicates no effects. There is always the possibility, of course, that the past two decades of educational innovation have tempered what would have been even more dramatic declines in achievement had no changes in the schools been made at all. On the other hand, there is always the possibility that student achievement would have risen had we not tried to tinker with the existing system. Although either of these explanations may be true, a more prudent reading of the evidence is that school reform simply has not done anything at all. How could this be? A number of explanations for its apparent failure may be suggested.

DO SCHOOLS REALLY MATTER?

One reading of the evidence on school reform and student achievement comes from those critics who contend that school reform hasn't worked because schools don't really matter. For example, if students' achievement were completely determined by other factors—their native intelligence, the quality of their home environment, how much television they watch, how much protein in their diets, whatever—no amount of change in school curriculum, instruction, or organization could make a difference. These critics argue that although it sometimes *looks* as if schools make a difference in student performance—because student achievement is higher in some schools and lower in others—what we often think of as "school effects" are more likely due to characteristics of the students themselves, and not to factors that schools have any control over.

Because good schools and good home environments so often go together, it has been extremely difficult for educational researchers to definitively state how much of the relative academic superiority of students who attend good schools is due to their schools, and how much of it is due to factors on which schools have no impact. Within the research community, the question has generated considerable debate but no certain conclusions, and answers have ranged from "schools don't make a difference at all, once family factors are taken into account" to "schools matter a good deal."

Why, after these many years of research, can we not answer this question definitively? Part of the difficulty stems from differences across studies in how schools are judged. Depending on the measure of school quality used, researchers come up with different conclusions. When very gross measures of school quality are used—the amount of money in the school's budget, for example, or the number of books in the school's library—research tends to show that differences in school quality are not important in predicting student achievement. It is this sort of finding that has buttressed the argument that schools don't really matter.

When finer measures of school quality are used, however—measures that look closely at the quality of classroom instruction—studies show that school practices can in fact make a difference, albeit a modest one. In one extensive program of research on young adolescents in London schools, for example, the researchers found that the overall climate of a school was significantly associated with student performance, attendance, and conduct, even after controlling for differences between the schools in student background and ability. Generally speaking, students behaved and performed better in schools where teachers were supportive but firm, and maintained high, well-defined standards for academic work. The London studies also found that the students performed better when they had better-prepared and better-organized teachers. In short, students score higher on tests of achievement when they have been taught by good teachers in good schools.

This hardly comes as a surprise. Anyone who has had both good teachers and bad teachers knows firsthand that a good teacher can bring out the best in a student, while a bad teacher can squelch even the most motivated student's desire to learn—so it is absurd to argue that the quality of teachers our students encounter isn't important. Similarly, anyone who has attended both good schools and bad schools can attest to the fact that it is easier to pay attention, remain motivated, and, as a consequence, learn in a school that is well-organized, well-equipped, and well-staffed than in a school that has few resources, is disorderly, and is administered by uncaring or poorly trained personnel. To argue, then, that schools don't matter *at all* flies in the face of experience, reason, and a fair amount of research.

THE LIBERAL ACCOUNT

A second account for the failure of school reform, popular among political liberals, is that schools matter, but that we haven't spent enough money on reforming them. According to this view, our attempts at changing America's schools simply have not been vigorous or extensive enough. Many educational reformers point to deficiencies in funding for school innovation, firmly believing that their programs would work if only they were adequately supported. Their argument is that school reform would work if we were willing to spend what it actually takes to change the ways in which our schools function. According to them, students are failing to achieve because schools do not provide sufficient opportunities to learn.

The argument that school reform hasn't succeeded because we haven't spent the necessary money is highly questionable. Currently, the United States spends far more per student than Japan or China, for example, whose students achieve far more than ours. In fact, America's schools spend more per pupil annually than virtually any of the countries that routinely trounce us in international scholastic comparisons. We may be spending money on the *wrong* things, but on the face of it, it would not appear that more spending in and of itself is the answer to America's achievement problems.

I grant that it is probably true that at the extreme low end of the funding distribution—that is, if we were to consider assisting only the nation's poorest school districts—providing additional resources might boost student achievement somewhat, so long as the resources were genuinely spent on enhancing opportunities to learn and not, as they generally have been, on administration and ancillary services. But increasing funding for our poorest school districts still would not address the larger problem of our *across-the-board* poor educational performance—it only offers the possibility of raising terrible schools closer to the ranks of the mediocre. Remember, the NAEP data show quite clearly that our achievement problem exists not only in our most impoverished school districts, but, as we have seen, in our most advantaged ones as well. Given considerable evidence from studies in this country of only a very modest relation between annual expenditures and student achievement, increasing spending in the average school district is unlikely to make much of a difference in student performance. Although the deplorable conditions that prevail in many poor inner-city and rural communities undoubtedly impede learning in these settings, it is difficult to believe that the poor achievement of students who attend school in well-funded, middle-class communities is due to their lacking sufficient opportunity to learn.

Perhaps more importantly, putting into place many of the more radically innovative school reforms that have been proposed or tried out only on a very small scale will require far more money than is likely to be available to most of the nation's school districts in the coming decade. We frequently read or hear about schools that have turned around student performance after a massive infusion of expertise and cash, but we do not hear about the failures—the schools in which achievement does not improve, despite the best intentions of philanthropists and educational reformers. But even still, the well-publicized demonstrations of innovative programs that receive so much media attention teach us what schools *might* be able to do if they were lavishly funded; what isn't reported very often is that when the lavish funding is scaled back, the observed improvements in student performance rapidly disappear.

Even if the school reformers are correct in complaining that their efforts have been underfunded—and we are not sure that this is true—their proposed modifications would cost substantially more than we have been willing or able to spend during the past two decades of educational reform and innovation. Adjusted for inflation, our current expenditures per pupil are higher than ever. And given the grim budgetary projections we read about daily, it is highly unlikely that federal, state, and local governments will be spending a great deal more money on school reform in the coming years than they were able to spend in the past ten; if anything, they will be spending less. Discussions about the potential efficacy of educational reforms that we can't afford are not going to solve our educational problems.

There is a variation on the "opportunities to learn" theme that warrants special consideration. This is the view that in order to provide adequate opportunities to learn, schools must first address the social problems—family dysfunction, drug use, poverty, teen pregnancy, violence, and so on—that interfere with student achievement. As these problems have grown more widespread, schools have been caught in a bind: On the one hand, if schools do not address them, students will not be able to be engaged in learning. On the other hand, however, if schools *do* address them—by providing counseling, social services, special programs, and the like—schools will be so strapped financially that they will not be able to fulfill their primary purpose: education.

Few social scientists today challenge the assertion that a large number of American adolescents, especially poor and minority youth living in inner cities and depressed rural areas, are afflicted with social and psychological problems that interfere with their ability to be engaged in school. In their 1993 book *Losing Generations*, for example, a blue-ribbon panel of the National Academy of Sciences estimated that more than one-quarter of all American young people are at serious risk for having difficulty making a successful transition into adulthood as a result of early out-of-wedlock pregnancy, failure to complete high school, criminal or delinquent behavior, substance abuse, or some combination of these and other factors.

The issue is not whether these problems exist (they clearly do), or whether they warrant national attention (they certainly do), but whether schools are the proper institutions through which these problems should be addressed. Although I accept the argument that schools are in a prime position to deliver psychological services to young people because they have ready access to the child and adolescent populations, the costs of turning educational institutions into social service agencies may well outweigh the benefits. Studies show quite persuasively that children achieve more when they attend schools that stress intellectual activities and are organized around a common purpose—quality education. Excessive involvement in social service delivery dilutes the school's energy and resources and leaves students, teachers, and parents confused about its mission.

Moreover, it is not at all clear that schools are especially effective at delivering nonacademic services, nor is it necessarily the case that the social problems afflicting America's young people are best addressed by intervening at the level of the individual student (which is, after all, what schools are set up to do). One could easily make the argument (and many social scientists, in fact, have) that the most effective approaches to dealing with the psychological and behavioral problems afflicting today's young people inhere in efforts to alter the families and communities in which students are raised. Schools may be able to deliver after-the-fact services (counseling, health care, nutritional services) to students who need them, but it is clear that if we hope to do anything more than provide psychological and social Band-Aids, we need preventive interventions on a much larger and comprehensive scale than schools can, or should, oversee.

THE CONSERVATIVE ACCOUNT

A different explanation has been offered by some educational reformers who believe that the failure of school reform is due to *how* schools have spent money they have been given, rather than deficiencies in how much money they have had to spend. Here the most familiar argument is that too much of schools' resources—money, personnel, and time—is dedicated to nonacademic services. These critics typically are more politically conservative and closely identified with the "back to basics, higher standards" camp of the school reform movement. They argue that we would see improvements in student achievement if we would only reorient our educational spending away from the frills, focusing instead on classroom instruction and holding everyone's feet to the fire.

The argument that the increased allocation of time and money away from academic instruction is the root cause of the decline in student achievement—or, more importantly, that reallocating resources back to academic instruction would reverse the trend—deserves careful consideration. If it is true, it suggests a way to turn American achievement around without spending additional dollars. Indeed, some conservative critics argue that eliminating a lot of the extras would simultaneously raise achievement and save money.

There is considerable evidence for the claim that our schools pay less attention to academic instruction today than they did in the past. For example, the proportion of school budgets that go to teacher salaries—as opposed to administrators and service personnel—has dropped dramatically, from nearly 60 percent of school budgets in the late 1950s to about 40 percent in the late 1980s. Research on how students spend time in school, by the National Education Commission on Time and Learning, points in a similar direction: Only 40 percent of students' school days are spent on academic subjects, far less than the comparable figure in other countries. Too much time, and too much money, the commission argued, is spent on personal growth, life skills, and nonessential subjects (i.e., subjects other than language arts, mathematics, science, and social studies). Too much of teachers' time, even in academic subject classes, is spent "off-task"—on student discipline and administrative paperwork. In most schools, too little is expected of students.

Though intuitively appealing, the back-to-basics approach to the current educational crisis overlooks an important bit of history, and in doing so, it confuses cause and effect, correlation with causation. The reallocation of resources away from academic instruction, much of which happened during the 1970s and 1980s, did not occur out of the blue. It took place against a backdrop of *already* declining academic achievement and rising student disengagement. The reallocation of resources occurred because of the growing perception among educators that American students needed these additional, nonacademic courses and services in order to remain engaged in school. In other words, schools moved away from a more basic approach to education precisely because of declining student achievement. The increased attention schools have paid to nonacademic matters has been as much a *response* to students' poor educational performance as a cause of it.

Consider, for example, some of the reforms of the late 1960s and early

1970s. Courses like "life skills" and career education were added to the school day specifically because educators hoped that a dose of relevance would help maintain student interest when their attention in academic courses seemed to be flagging. Courses in personal growth—aimed at raising self-esteem or enhancing social skills—were added largely because experts felt that student achievement was suffering because of deficiencies in these realms. Courses in sex education, drug education, and family relationships were added in part because it was felt that the problems youngsters had in these areas were interfering with their academic achievement and that families were not addressing them adequately. These curricular changes may have had other, perhaps beneficial, effects (e.g., more real-world smarts, higher self-esteem, more knowledge about contraception), but we should not confuse the consequences of these programs with the reasons for their introduction.

If, as I believe it to be, these nonacademic additions to the curriculum were reactions to, and not antecedents of, a lack of student interest, there is little reason to suspect that removing them from the curriculum will have a major positive impact on student achievement. Given the absence of evidence that these nonacademic programs improved students' performance in academic areas, we can probably remove nonacademic programs from the curriculum without seeing a deleterious impact on student achievement, and we may realize some financial savings in the process. But we should not expect to see an upturn in student performance just because students will have to spend a relatively higher proportion of their time in academic classes. Students were already beginning to be disengaged *before* nonacademic classes began to dominate the school's curriculum, during the time when schools' offerings were in fact dominated by the "basics." Depressing as it may be to admit, returning the curriculum back to basics, in all likelihood, will not itself affect student achievement very much.

What about the comparisons between our schools and those in other countries where achievement is higher—comparisons that suggest that students in classrooms abroad spend more time on academic subjects and more days in school than American students? Doesn't this provide convincing evidence that the root cause of our achievement problem is that American schooling is neither intensive enough nor sufficiently focused on academic matters? Not necessarily—again, we should be careful about mistaking correlation for causation. Although the international studies tell us that demanding schools and student achievement often go hand in hand, they do not indicate that the former actually causes the latter. As we shall see, there are other differences between youngsters' lives in America and elsewhere that may account for the achievement gap.

TOWARD A MORE SENSIBLE VISION OF WHAT SCHOOLS CAN REALISTICALLY ACCOMPLISH

Thus far, I have argued against both the liberal position that schools simply need to provide more opportunities for students to learn and the conservative position that our academic ills will be cured if only schools would return to basics and tougher standards. Each of these positions is partially true, but each is also terribly inadequate. The ongoing political debate over whether schools should focus relatively more on providing increased opportunities to learn, or relatively more on implementing and enforcing higher standards, is the wrong debate, for it begins from the questionable assumption that changing schools in one direction or the other will, in and of itself, result in improved student performance. A change in either direction will, in my view, lead to no appreciable changes in student achievement at all. Moreover, continuing to debate the relative merits of the liberal versus the conservative approaches to school reform deflects attention from the real problem.

Our research indicates that a profitable discussion about the declining achievement of American youngsters should begin by examining students' lives *outside* of school. Let us agree that students need schools that provide both opportunities to learn as well as standards to live up to, and that schools can and should provide both. But our study also shows that school is only one of many influences—and probably, when all is said and done, not even the most important one—that affect what students learn and how well they perform on tests of achievement. It seems only fair to acknowledge, based on studies of school quality and its relation to student performance, as well as disappointing evaluations of many, many different types of school reform, that, although schools matter, they probably account for less variation in student achievement than we believe—or than we hope—they do.

When research shows, as it generally does, that school reform has not paid off in improved achievement, we should not take this as a sign that schools don't matter, or even that they only matter a little bit. Rather, we should use this observation as an impetus to look at the broader context in which our children are educated and to understand how schools are linked to other forces in students' lives.

Does this mean that we should not include school quality in discussions of how best to reverse the achievement decline? Of course not. But it does suggest that a more productive inquiry into causes of poor student achievement might begin by acknowledging that any influence that schools might have—however strong or weak—occurs against a backdrop of other factors in students' lives. As a consequence, we cannot understand whether (or, more importantly, how) schools make a difference without taking into account the other forces in youngsters' lives that either diminish or amplify the effects of school. Rather than asking whether schools make a difference, or how much of a difference they make, we should be asking, "What conditions need to be in place so that schools *can* make a difference?"

School reform is not doomed to failure, but, as you will read, changes in other facets of students' lives must occur before school reform is to yield any major benefits. Unless and until we are willing to address these other factors, school reform—whether liberal or conservative in its bent, limited or overarching in its scope—will not succeed. In the ongoing debate over how we should respond to the low achievement of American students—whether schools should provide more opportunities for learning or more rigorous expectations—I think we have framed the question around the wrong issue. The discussion has focused on schools, when it should have focused on students.

NATURE, NURTURE, AND SCHOOL ACHIEVEMENT

It is important at this juncture, especially in light of the ongoing and heated debate over the relative importance of heredity and environment as influences on intelligence, to address the issue of native intelligence and the extent to which achievement is genetically determined and therefore out of the reach of schools. It is important to be absolutely clear that the reason schools matter less than we wish they would is not because student achievement is genetically determined, but because schools are only one small part of the environment in which student achievement develops and is expressed.

Most social scientists familiar with the literature on genes, environment, and IQ agree that individual variability in intelligence-test performance is due both to genetic and environmental factors, and that observed differences in individual IQs are perhaps as much as 50 to 60 percent due to genetic differences between individuals. But we should be extremely cautious about generalizing from studies of IQ-test performance to studies of academic achievement. The links between IQ and school performance, while significant, are far less strong than most people imagine. As I discuss in a later chapter, there are a great many factors that combine with, and interact with, intelligence in influencing students' grades and achievement-test scores, and IQ is a very small part of the overall equation.

Indeed, when one takes into account the proportion of intelligence that is *not* genetically determined and combines this information with data on the proportion of achievement that is *not* determined by intelligence, it is quite clear that individual differences in school achievement are unlikely to be due mainly to differences in genes. Indeed, studies directly assessing this issue show that school achievement (unlike performance on IQ tests) is far more influenced by environmental factors than by genetic ones. Moreover, no genetic account could explain the across-the-board decline in achievement-test performance that has taken place in the past thirty years, since this is far too short a time period in which to see any genetic effects. If we wish to understand this recent historical change, we must look to our environment, not to our genes, for explanations. But we must broaden what we look at in the environment, going beyond the school itself.

If recent attempts at school reform appear to have failed, in the sense that they have not lifted student achievement, it is not because achievement is genetically fixed, nor is it because school reform efforts have been misguided or underfunded. Research shows quite convincingly that academic achievement is not fixed by heredity. And many attempts at changing our schools have been well founded and well funded, and most have been based on solid educational research. Unfortunately, however, even the most well-intentioned, well-thought-out plan for changing our schools will not succeed unless we look at the problem of student achievement in a broader context.

What has changed in the past three decades—the period during which our achievement problem became most severe—has not been our schools, but our students' lives outside of school. As a consequence of these transformations, today's schools and teachers face a cohort of students who come to school less interested, less motivated, and less engaged in the business of learning. In the chapters that follow, you will come to understand how these problems—problems in students' attitudes, values, and beliefs about the importance of education—underlie the current crisis in American education.

A DIFFERENT POINT OF VIEW

In this book, I offer a different perspective on America's achievement problem that I hope will stimulate discussion among parents, educators, and educational policy-makers—indeed, among all citizens. In the chapters that follow, I shall argue that neither the source of our achievement problem, nor the mechanism through which we can best address it, is to be found by examining or altering our schools. Accordingly, this book will rankle those educators who have an unshakable belief in the power of schools to effect major changes in the academic performance of students. At the same time, however, it will support those educators who feel, as many of them understandably do, that they have been unfairly held responsible for our students' academic deficiencies.

Should we continue to think carefully about matters such as curriculum, school organization, and teacher training? Of course we should. Improvements in these domains may well have small, but nonetheless important, consequences for our students—and given the current achievement crisis facing America, we cannot afford to turn our nation's nose up at even small improvements. But in most school districts across the country—outside of the obviously compromised districts serving exceedingly disadvantaged youngsters in inner cities and rural areas—the facilities, curriculum, organization, and level of teacher competence is probably adequate to the task of educating our children. If we can agree that simply improving the average school will have, at best, only modest results, we are at least on the road toward a more realistic vision of what schools can do and a more sensible approach to the problem of American student underachievement. Many of the findings of our study help explain why the past decade of "back to basics"–style reform has been as disappointing in its results as the "make school attractive" reforms of the 1970s.

The contention that today's students are less engaged in the business of education than their counterparts were in previous generations is neither fresh nor particularly profound—as almost anyone who has set foot in an American school in the past decade would attest. Where I differ from other commentators who have reached similar conclusions is not in my assessment of the problem, but in my view of how best to respond to it. Specifically, I take issue with the usual response: that because today's students are somehow different from their predecessors, schools must find ways of responding to, adapting to, or catering to this changed clientele. If the failed school reform attempts of the last two decades teach us anything, it is that trying to fix our achievement problem by expanding the nonacademic offerings of schools, as a means of making school more "attractive" to students, is destined to failure. These palliative measures only exacerbate the achievement problem by draining resources away from high-quality academic instruction in the classroom.

Changing our schools to respond to a less interested, less motivated, less focused student populace does little to address the basic underlying problem—the lack of student engagement. Thus, we must come to a clearer understanding not only of what schools need to do to engage apathetic students, but of why students come to school with such low levels of interest and enthusiasm in the first place. In order to do this, and, accordingly, in order to reengage students in school, we must focus our attention not on the classroom, not on the principal's office, not on the school district's administration, but on students themselves. No degree of school reform, no matter how carefully planned, will be successful in solving the achievement problem unless we first face and resolve the engagement problem.

FOUR

Disengaged Students

Ten years ago, I firmly believed that America's teenagers were little different, as a group, from those of previous generations. I felt it was my obligation as an expert on adolescent development familiar with the scientific study of adolescence, and as an advocate of young people, to help the media "dedramatize" adolescence. Far too much was being made, it seemed to me, of the problems of young people. More attention needed to be paid to the fact that the vast majority of adolescents were growing up healthy and untroubled.

Today, I am far less sanguine about the state of our youth. There are too many indications that today's young people are significantly more troubled than their counterparts were previously, and that their troubles are both deeper and more prevalent across the population. This is nowhere more evident than in our nation's classrooms, where an extraordinarily high percentage of students appear to be alienated and disengaged.

I know full well that adults always have a tendency to look at the upcoming generation of teenagers and see them as troubled, disrespectful, difficult—just as my parents viewed my friends and me when we were teenagers in the 1960s, and just as today's teenagers will view their own adolescent children when they are parents twenty years from now. Any student of the history of adolescence knows that a certain amount of intergenerational conflict has been present throughout time and is inevitable. So, when I say that it seems that today's teenagers are more disengaged than they have been in the recent past, I do so with an acute awareness of the inclination for adults to look at youth negatively. But there are objective data—from national surveys as well as in our own study—that indicate that a larger number of young people today are disconnected from school.

As I noted in the last chapter, we emphasized disengagement from school in our research because it is both a cause and a symptom of other difficulties that adolescents are having in their lives. It is a cause of these problems because school plays such an important role in structuring youngsters' lives; when youngsters are not engaged in school, they lose a large amount of the psychological structure that holds their day together. At the same time, because school is so important an organizing principle in adolescents' lives, chronic academic alienation may be indicative of deeper, more pervasive problems—just as chronic difficulties at work may be indicative of deeper problems for an adult.

For these reasons, we should not look at disengagement from school as simply an educational problem—although it obviously has important educational implications—but as a more general barometer of adolescent malaise. In fact, studies clearly show that lack of interest in school is highly correlated with other, more worrisome indicators of teenage difficulty, including drug and alcohol use, depression, delinquency, and sexual precocity—in the language of psychologists, disengagement from school is part of a "syndrome" of problem behavior.

The emphasis in our research has been on understanding factors in the student's life that allow him or her to become engaged in school, rather than on factors in the school that do or do not interest students. Engagement in school is a two-way street—schools need to be interesting, but students need to be willing and able to be interested. While schools and teachers differ in how engaging they are, most discussions of contemporary education overemphasize the responsibility of school to be engaging and ignore the obligation of the student to be "engageable." Indeed, our exclusive focus on how to make schools more engaging is one of the central problems of the school reform movement.

Something has happened during the past quarter century that has led to the widespread alienation of youngsters from school—even youngsters whose family backgrounds would have predicted otherwise. School was once accepted by virtually all middle-class youngsters as the most important focus of their life, and few of these children questioned the value of school or the need to perform well there. Now, it seems, a large number of these students thumb their collective nose at their teachers, view school as a nuisance, and place school low, if not at the absolute bottom, of their list of priorities. One goal of our study was to find out how extensive this alienation is and understand its origins and correlates. Before I turn to this issue, however, a few words are necessary about the distinction between ability and engagement.

ABILITY OR ENGAGEMENT?

Although we can easily distinguish between engaged and disengaged students just by observing them in a classroom, surprisingly little research has examined the role of engagement in student achievement. Far more research has focused on the cognitive, or intellectual, determinants of achievement than on the emotional and social ones. This imbalance is reflected both in the way we typically account for individual differences in student achievement (students who score higher on tests of achievement are simply labeled "smarter") and in the ways in which we tend to explain group differences in achievement (one group scores higher than another because the first group is "brighter"). When we discuss students and their performance in school, we speak in the language of ability. Instead, we should be speaking in the language of engagement.

This is not to say, of course, that ability plays no role in influencing how children perform in school. But while factors such as intelligence obviously play a role in influencing achievement, our disproportionate interest in these factors has diverted our attention away from the many noncognitive factors that are just as, if not more, important. No amount of cognitive ability will result in actual achievement if the requisite emotional characteristics that contribute to interest in school are not present.

There is another good reason why we should pay more attention to emotional and social influences on achievement than we presently do. Given the modest size of the correlation between intelligence and achievement, there must be variables other than intelligence that affect how well a student performs in school. Grades in school are only modestly correlated with scores on standardized tests of intelligence, and scores on intelligence tests are even less highly correlated with how far individuals go in their schooling. If you were to display school performance as a pie chart, showing how different influences contributed to levels of accomplishment, you would find that ability takes up a relatively small slice of the pie, with much of the pie left over for other factors to explain. Factors that are outside the realm of cognitive ability necessarily must play a critically important role in influencing a given student's record of achievement.

Another reason for looking at factors outside of ability in understanding student achievement is historical, and is related to our earlier look at the decline or stagnation in achievement test scores that has taken place over the past three decades. As I noted, today's students, on average, know less than their counterparts did twenty-five years ago. But while today's students are less *knowledgeable* (as measured on tests of achievement), are they actually less *intelligent* (as measured on IQ tests)?

The answer is no. If anything, studies suggest that the average intelligence of the population has been *increasing*, not decreasing, over time, most likely as a result of improvements in early nutrition, prenatal care, and health, all of which affect IQ-test performance for the better. Despite the widespread belief that Americans have gotten "dumber," there is no evidence to suggest that they have—at least with respect to the sorts of skills measured on standardized intelligence tests. What Americans have become is not less intelligent, but less interested in being educated. In concrete terms, although today's students appear less interested in school than they were in previous generations, they are no less smart.

Because we know that students' achievement-test scores declined and have remained stagnant during the same time period in which their intelligence was either stable or on the rise, then changes in *noncognitive* factors must have played a major role in the across-the-board drop in achievement that occurred during the past three decades. What this means is that any discussion of student achievement—whether we are talking about a parent's assessment of his or her child's school performance, a teacher's evaluation of how an entire class is doing, or a national study of how our country's students are faring—must include a systematic consideration of the noncognitive factors that affect student performance.

Unfortunately, most research to date has told us very little about student engagement—about the relative proportions of engaged and disengaged students in our nation's classrooms, about the ways in which engagement is turned into achievement, about the determinants of high-versus-low school engagement within the adolescent population, or about the degree to which a student's level of engagement can be altered. We do know, however, that engagement must be a prerequisite to learning, and, consequently, that any discussion of student achievement—whether the discussion concerns how to help an individual student do better in school, how to foster greater achievement in a classroom, or understanding why some groups of individuals achieve more than others—must begin with a discussion of student engagement.

In our research, we attempted to directly measure the behavioral and emotional components of school engagement. All told, we performed the most comprehensive assessment of students' actual investment in the day-to-day process of schooling that has ever been conducted.

HOW ENGAGED STUDENTS BEHAVE

It is surprisingly difficult to assess students' engagement in terms of their behavior inside and outside of school, at least in the contemporary United States. Compared with other countries, our schools expect relatively little from students. Our school day is not especially long, and most of it—about 60 percent, according to national studies—is spent in nonacademic activities, including study halls, ancillary classes, and break times. The amount of homework assigned in most schools is minimal, and students are given ample time in class and during free periods to complete their assigned homework before the school day ends. As a consequence, there are few opportunities for students to demonstrate exceptional levels of engagement, and not that many ways of distinguishing between interested and uninterested students on the basis of their behavior alone.

Nevertheless, we felt that it was important to have some indicators of engagement based on students' actual behavior in school rather than limiting our assessment to their attitudes and beliefs. Accordingly, we asked a series of questions of students that measured their compliance with school's demands on their time and energy, however slight these demands actually are. These questions concerned patterns of class attendance and class-cutting, whether students completed the homework they were assigned, the amount of time students spent on homework in each academic subject class, how hard students tried during their classes, whether students who were given choices took challenging classes or easy ones, and whether students do things like cheat on tests or turn in work that is not their own. By our liberal definition (liberal because of the low expectations schools place on students), engaged students attend their classes, try reasonably hard to do well in them, complete the homework they are assigned, and don't cheat. In contrast, disengaged students cut class regularly, exert little effort in the classroom, take easier classes, fail to do the work that is assigned to them, and break school rules concerning cheating.

What did our study reveal about levels of student engagement according to these indicators? The overall pattern suggests that an extremely large proportion of students—somewhere around 40 percent—are just going through the motions. (Our study was conducted during the late 1980s and early 1990s, but we have little reason to believe that circumstances are markedly different today; if anything, they have probably worsened in the past several years.) The stereotyped portrayals of disenfranchised teenagers in the classroom that we have become so accustomed to seeing in film and on television are not, it turns out, exaggerations. True, most students report that they attend classes regularly—only about 10 percent cut classes routinely—and well over 80 percent say they would stay in school even if they were able to secure a good full-time job. But at the same time, it is clear that when they are in school, a large proportion of students are physically present but psychologically absent. According to their own reports, between one-third and 40 percent of students say that when they are in class, they are neither trying very hard nor paying attention. Two-thirds say they have cheated on a test in the past year. Nine out of ten report that they have copied someone else's homework.

For some students (about 20 percent) disengagement from school is due in part to confusion, especially, students say, in math and science classes (which, interestingly, students rate as more challenging than other classes). So, there are some students who tune out mainly because they cannot keep up. But for many more, disengagement is not a reaction to too much pressure or to classes that are too difficult, but a response to having too little demanded of them and to the absence of any consequences for failing to meet even these minimal demands.

How little are our students pushed? According to our research and other national surveys, the majority of high school students in the United States spend four or fewer hours per week on homework. Only one in six spends ten or more hours each week—that is, the equivalent of two hours on each school day—studying outside of school. When placed alongside data on the low proportion of time students spend *in school* on academic matters—considerably less than half the school day is spent on academic subjects—the picture that emerges is alarming.

What are students doing with their time outside of school, if they are not doing homework? According to our survey and to other systematic studies of adolescent time use, the most time-consuming activity is "hanging out" with friends. A close runner-up for many is working at a part-time job. In later chapters, we'll look more closely at these two activities—socializing and paid employment—and the toll they are taking on student achievement in this country. For now, keep in mind that international comparisons show that students in other countries spend considerably more time on their studies outside of school (in some countries, in fact, up to five times the amount that American students do) and significantly less time hanging out with friends and in part-time work. If we really want to understand why our students fare so much worse on tests of achievement than their foreign counterparts, perhaps we should be looking less at differences in our countries' schools, and more at differences in our teenagers' lives.

It is tempting to turn these findings around and point them squarely at our schools—that is, to fault schools for having low standards and minimal expectations, and to see these factors as the *causes* of low student engagement and poor achievement. To frame the problem this way, however, misses an important part of the story; namely, that the minimal demands and low expectations characteristic of most schools developed partly in response to low student engagement. True enough, the combination of low engagement and low standards creates a vicious circle—students disengage from school, schools demand less from disengaged students, students disengage further when little is demanded of them, and so on. But to ask schools to shoulder the full blame is to disregard the impact that student disengagement has on school practices.

Let me illustrate this point by drawing on a fascinating study of teacher expectations and student employment authored some years ago by Linda McNeil. Instead of asking how students were affected by having after-school jobs—a question I take up in a later chapter—McNeil asked how teachers were affected by having a large number of their students work. What McNeil found, interestingly, is that teachers lower their expectations for student performance in response to student disengagement from school. "The more students worked, and for longer hours," McNeil wrote, "the less some teachers required of them at school. The more school became boring and less demanding, the more students increased their work hours."

Of course, it is appealing to blame teachers and schools for not demanding enough from their students; this is a central tenet in the conservative school reform movement. But it is not likely that leniency on the part of schools is the ultimate source of the problem. Teachers, in many respects, are reacting to the disengagement of their students and, as we shall see in a later chapter, to the low standards set by students' parents. Thus, while it is true that very little homework is assigned in American schools, this is partly because students often do not do what their teachers ask of them: More than a third of the students we surveyed say they do not do the homework they are given. And as for students spending a large part of their school day on nonacademic matters, at least some of this is due to students being given choices concerning how they spend their time in school, and not choosing academic activities. We can, and should, blame schools for giving students the opportunity to select less demanding classes, but we should not blame schools for the fact that students are all too willing to take schools up on their offer.

THE EMOTIONS OF ENGAGEMENT

Because expectations for student behavior are so low, it isn't very difficult for a large percentage of students to meet them and, as a consequence, to appear "engaged enough." Thus, any assessment of student engagement that is based exclusively on whether students are doing what is expected of them may paint a more positive picture of life in America's high schools than is really the case (e.g., the good news is that two-thirds of students say they do the homework they are assigned; the bad news is that doing all of their assigned homework takes students less than one hour each day). In order to get a better grasp of just how connected students are to the activities and purposes of school, we also studied their emotions—their motives, values, and attitudes.

Emotionally, students differ in how hard they strive to succeed, in how positively they feel about school, and in how positively they feel about themselves when they are in the student role. At the most engaged end of the continuum are students who are interested in doing well in school because they have a strong intrinsic motivation to achieve, because succeeding in the classroom makes them feel proud and accomplished, and because they connect success in school with success in other aspects of life. These students enjoy going to school, and they easily become immersed in classroom activities. For whatever reason, they are committed to their education.

At the other end of the continuum are students who are emotionally disconnected from school. These students have a low need for achievement, what we might call a weak work ethic, and a negative orientation toward school. They complain about school being boring or irrelevant or repetitive, and they are easily distracted from classroom activity. When these students are in school, their mood tends to be negative, and school demands feel more like nuisances than opportunities to demonstrate what they are capable of.

We measured the emotional side of school engagement in a number of different ways. One of our most important measures was a scale that tapped what we call "work orientation"—how much effort individuals exert in the face of difficulty and how much pride they take in the successful completion of tasks. For instance, we asked students to agree or disagree with statements such as "I find it hard to stick to anything that takes a long time to do" or "I tend to go from one thing to another before finishing any one of them." Students who strongly agree with these sorts of sentiments have an extremely low work orientation.

Our work orientation scale captures students' attitudes toward hard work—is hard work something to tackle, or is it something to shy away from? Another important part of the emotional side of engagement is the student's attitude toward school itself. Emotionally engaged students try hard in school, believe that doing well in school is important, and have faith that what they are learning there is valuable. We used a measure of "school orientation" that asked students to endorse or disagree with such items as "I feel satisfied with school because I'm learning a lot" or "The best way to get through most days at school is to goof off with my friends."

Our survey also included a number of specific questions about students' day-to-day emotional state in the classroom—how hard they concentrate, how distracted they are in class, how closely they pay attention, and so on. We asked these questions for each major subject area (English, math, science, and social studies), and then averaged them for each student, so that we could take into account the fact that students' moods and feelings vary from class to class or from teacher to teacher. By averaging answers across different sorts of classes and different teachers, we could make sure that a student's profile wasn't unduly influenced by one particular subject or teacher.

The information we collected on the emotional side of engagement presents a disturbing picture. More than one-third of the students we surveyed showed signs of being emotionally disengaged from school, as indexed by measures of mind-wandering, lack of interest, or inattentiveness. Half of the students we surveyed say their classes are boring. A third say they have lost interest in school, that they are not learning very much, and that they get through the school day by fooling around with their classmates. And remember, ours was a sample of "average" students in "average" American schools—not a sample of "high-risk" youngsters in "high-risk" school settings.

We cannot say with certainty whether this emotional disengagement is a cause or an effect of the lack of commitment to academics we see when we look at students' behavior—the small amount of time spent on studies, the disdain for academic classes, and so on. In all likelihood, it is a circular process: when students aren't interested in school, they devote little energy to school pursuits; over time, the less energy students devote to school, the less invested they feel in the activity. But whatever the account, it is clear that for a very large proportion of students in this country, school is little more than a gathering place where they congregate in order to mingle with their friends. Within the context of this marvelous party, classes are annoyances to be endured, just so many interruptions in the course of a busy day of socializing.

THE BELIEFS BEHIND DISENGAGEMENT

In the best of all educational worlds, the activities of school would be of sufficient intrinsic interest to engage students on this basis alone—students would strive to learn because the process of learning was psychologically fulfilling and the resulting sense of mastery was personally rewarding. We have all had learning experiences in which we felt this way—energized, invigorated, caught up in the sheer pleasure that comes from mastering something challenging and difficult. It is one of the most satisfying feelings there is.

While there are no doubt times in school when learning is intrinsically motivating, it doesn't happen often for the vast majority of students, especially once they have reached adolescence. Most of the time, what keeps students going in school is not intrinsic motivation—motivation derived from the process of learning itself—but extrinsic motivation—motivation that comes from the real or perceived consequences associated with success or failure, whether these consequences are immediate (in the form of grades, the reactions of parents, or the responses of friends) or delayed (in the form of anticipated impact in other educational settings or in the adult world of work).

In order to be emotionally engaged in school, students must believe that what they are learning there is either interesting or valuable—and preferably, both. This does not mean that they must find every lesson, every assignment, and every bit of information communicated in class absolutely riveting. But in order to become and remain engaged in school, students must have some sense that what they are doing on a daily basis holds some value—that as a result of being engaged and exerting effort, they will acquire some bit of useful knowledge, learn an important skill, or grow in some way that is fulfilling, satisfying, or personally meaningful.

Researchers who study human motivation have spent considerable time examining the relative importance of intrinsic versus extrinsic motivation in promoting learning and success in school. We know that early on—in preschool, for example—children are highly intrinsically motivated and nat urally curious, and that they need little in the way of extrinsic rewards to motivate them to participate energetically in classroom activities. We also know, however, that it is possible to undermine children's intrinsic motivation by giving them extrinsic rewards for things that they had previously found intrinsically interesting. Thus, for example, if you were to take an ac-tivity that an individual finds intrinsically satisfying but for which there are no extrinsic rewards—playing a musical instrument as a hobby, for exam-ple—and you were to begin to reward the individual extrinsically for engag-ing in the activity (for instance, you began paying the individual for practicing the instrument), the individual's intrinsic interest in the endeavor would actually decline somewhat, and he or she might then require extrin-sic rewards to remain engaged in the activity. With time, when we are re-warded extrinsically for doing something that holds natural intrinsic interest, we begin to lose some of that intrinsic interest and become more dependent on extrinsic rewards to motivate our performance.

Over the course of their educational careers, students are increasingly exposed to extrinsic rewards for schoolwork. In preschool classrooms, for ex-ample, students tend to be praised more or less unconditionally and do not have their "work" evaluated by teachers. As children progress into and through elementary school, however, they start to be evaluated—first with comments and corrections, then with actual grades. Over time, these evalu-ations come to take on increasing importance, as students become aware that their parents and classmates are paying attention to the marks they earn and the comments their work elicits from teachers. One theory about what happens to students over time is that as the importance of extrinsic rewards increases over the course of elementary school, students' intrinsic interest in learning is progressively weakened. That is, as grades and other concrete consequences of school performance become more important and more salient, the intrinsic reward of learning is eroded.

By the time the average child has reached adolescence, he or she has been bombarded with enough messages about the extrinsic consequences of success or failure in school to undo most of the intrinsic motivation to learn that had been present in earlier periods of development. For most high school students, the main motivators of effort are grades (both for what they may bring in immediate rewards and because of their importance to college admission) and how success or failure would influence students' relations with their friends and their parents. Regardless of what parents and teachers *wish*, intrinsic motivation plays a relatively small role in motivating student performance in adolescence and beyond. In our survey, for example, the most common reason students gave for trying hard in school was not genuine interest in the material, but getting good grades in order to get into college.

I think it is important to listen closely to what students tell us about what motivates them to do well in school. It is important that educators continue to search for ways of making learning intrinsically motivating, but given what we know about the motivational histories of students once they have reached high school, it is equally important that students believe that success in school has extrinsic rewards as well. Students will not remain engaged in school unless they think that academic success will have a future payoff, either in terms of success in subsequent school settings, achievement in the workplace, increased earnings, or some combination of all three. If students believe that the academic side of school is merely an unpleasant obligation—that their time there need be spent on little more than "going through the motions"—and that whether they succeed or fail in school is largely irrelevant to their future, they will invest little time or energy in the educational process.

Much has been written about the declining fortunes of the current generation of young people and, in particular, about their grim prospects for economic success as young adults (at least, compared with the economic success enjoyed by prior generations). Some observers argue that one reason for the diminished investment of today's adolescents in school is that they have less faith than previous generations in the likely payoff of academic success. The lack of engagement in school of so many students may thus be viewed as a perfectly rational response. If students believe that doing well in school holds no appreciable benefit, they will be less inclined to direct their energies toward academics and likely to value other activities (such as social-izing or working at a part-time job) more highly.

We spent considerable effort assessing students' beliefs about the likely payoff of school success. We asked a series of questions about how strongly students believed that success in the workplace depended on doing well in school, and how confident they were that success in school actually would lead to a better or higher-paying job. We also asked questions about the con-sequences of *not* doing well in school, in order to see if adolescents felt that a lack of success would be a hindrance in the labor force.

Our analysis of their answers to these questions was quite illuminating. Do students believe in the benefits of schooling? Yes and no. Students be-lieve in the benefits associated with getting a diploma or a degree, but they are skeptical about the benefits associated with either learning or doing well in class. In other words, students believe that their success in the labor force will depend on the number of years of school they complete—they correctly believe that college graduates stand a better chance of getting good jobs than high school graduates, who, in turn, stand a better chance of occupational success than dropouts. At the same time, however, they do not associate later success either with *doing well* in school (in terms of their grades or the eval-uations of their teachers) or with *learning* what schools have to teach. In stu-dents' eyes, then, what matters is only whether one graduates—not how well one does or what one learns along the way.

If this is the prevailing belief among contemporary students—and our study suggests that it is—it is easy to understand why so many students coast through school without devoting much energy to their schoolwork. In their minds, there is little reason to exert themselves any more than is ab-solutely necessary to avoid failing, being held back, or not graduating. Within a belief system in which all that counts is graduation—in which earning good grades is seen as equivalent to earning mediocre ones, or worse yet, in which learning something from school is seen as unimportant—stu-dents choose the path of least resistance. And because schools hesitate to give students bad grades, hold them back, or fail to graduate them, students believe, with some accuracy, that there are no real consequences of doing poorly in school, as long as their performance is not poor enough to threaten graduation. Under these conditions, getting by, rather than striving to succeed, becomes the operating principle behind most students' behavior.

Our findings suggest that it would be possible to motivate students through grading practices, but only if the grades individuals earned had some real-world significance.

In psychological terms, it appears that students are motivated much more to avoid the negative consequences of failure than to reap the positive rewards of success. To the extent that this is true, then, students' behavior in school will depend more on how easy or difficult schools make it for students to fail than on how easy or difficult they make it for students to succeed. Thus, the easier it is for students to avoid the negative consequences of failure, the less effort they will exert in school. The problem, of course, is that under the present system of expectations and requirements—a system that has such low expectations and such minimal requirements that few students really fail—we have lost the ability to motivate students to work hard.

How might we respond to this dilemma? I have three suggestions.

One option is to raise the minimum standards and expectations in schools and to have genuine and unpleasant consequences for students who fail to meet them. Many educational reformers have called for raising schools' standards, but in the absence of making changes in the consequences to students of failing to meet the revised standards, the change in expectations alone will do little to improve student engagement or achievement—it will only frustrate teachers, since the gap between what they are asked to demand and what students actually do will widen. If we go the route of raising minimum standards, then, we must be prepared to respond to students who do not meet the standards.

A second option, not incompatible with the first, is to change the parameters of success. As it stands now, success in school, as indexed by levels of achievement and school performance, matters only for the small minority of students who seek admission to the nation's most selective colleges and universities. For the vast majority of students, who do not aspire toward or end up in these selective institutions, mediocre grades and a poor education are just as likely to lead to success as are good grades and a good education. One of the problems we must face squarely, then, is that we provide very little incentive for students to perform at an exceptional level. Our institutions of higher education are so eager to fill their classrooms that virtually anyone who can afford to go to college is guaranteed admission—witness the huge proportion of students admitted into universities who require some sort of remedial education (by most estimates, close to 40 percent of all entering freshmen). Unfortunately, the same orientation that characterizes student motivation in high school—do only what it takes to avoid failure and qualify for graduation—is true of most college students as well. At the college level, as in high school, the only students who strive for exceptional performance are those who are seeking admission to highly selective graduate and professional schools—a small minority of the total college population. One possibility, then, is to raise college entrance requirements at the majority of postsecondary institutions (i.e., not only at historically selective institutions) so that college admission is not guaranteed to students simply because they have completed high school.

There is a third option, and one that we should consider seriously along with the first two. We can try to alter the ways in which students are motivated—try to find ways to make them more oriented toward genuinely succeeding in school rather than merely avoiding the negative consequences of failing to graduate. Shifting students' orientation in this fashion will require not only changing students' attitudes and beliefs, but changing the behavior of their parents, their peers, and the larger society. Until the individuals in the adolescent's life value and reward success in school—by success, I mean not simply graduating from school, but excelling academically—we cannot expect the adolescent to strive for more than just getting by.

What does it take to motivate adolescents to strive for excellence in school? Given the overall climate I have just described—a climate in which schools expect little, penalize virtually nothing, and reward even the barest of achievements—what distinguishes those students who really exert themselves from those who merely try to get by? Our research points to clear and consistent differences in the home, peer, and extracurricular environments of engaged and disengaged students. As I detail in the chapters that follow, we have been able to identify the most important factors in students' lives *outside* of school that affect their attitudes, behavior, and performance *inside* school—factors that, if altered, would significantly improve American students' achievement.

We begin our discussion of these issues with a very sensitive topic: ethnic differences in student achievement and engagement.

FIVE

Ethnicity and Adolescent Achievement

One of the many strengths of our study was the ethnic variety in our sample. Unlike most research on adolescent development, which is based on samples of White youngsters (and middle-class White youngsters at that), our sample is ethnically and socioeconomically heterogeneous. Research on such varied populations is extremely important because, by the end of this century, ethnic minority youth will make up about one-third of the adolescent population. Although our sample was not deliberately recruited to reflect exactly the national population of teenagers, more than one-third of the participants in our study were minority youth, approximately evenly divided among youngsters from African-American, Asian-American, and Hispanic-American families.

Although we did not intend our study to focus primarily on ethnic differences in achievement and other aspects of adolescent development, we were struck repeatedly by how significant a role ethnicity played in structuring young people's lives, both inside and outside of school. Youngsters' patterns of activities, interests, and friendships were all influenced by their ethnic background. Moreover, we could not ignore the fact that students from different ethnic groups experienced markedly different degrees of success and failure in school. Like other investigators, we found that students of Asian descent are doing far better in school than are members of other ethnic groups, and that Black and Latino adolescents are doing significantly worse. We cannot attribute these patterns simply to ethnic differences in socioeconomic status—even *within* a specific social class, Asian students outperform White students, who in turn outperform Black and Latino students. This is not to say, of course, that there aren't plenty of exceptions to this pattern—Asians who are doing poorly, and Black and Latino students who are doing very well. But the general pattern of ethnic differences was marked and consistent across the nine schools we studied.

Venturing into the realm of ethnic differences in achievement is a difficult and delicate matter today, with racial divisions in this country at an extremely high level, and with heated and often uninformed debates in the popular press about genetic bases for ethnic and racial differences in intelligence and behavior. There will be readers who will be angry at what I say, if not simply at my colleagues and me studying ethnicity and achievement at all. That ethnic differences in achievement persist even after we take into account differences in social class only makes matters worse, because this suggests that the patterns cannot be dismissed as mere reflections of differences in economic resources. But our findings on ethnicity and achievement are just too important to ignore. Moreover, as you will read, they inform the more general issue of the declining achievement of American youth. Until we really understand the causes of this problem, we will not be able to solve it.

A FEW WORDS ABOUT ETHNICITY

A few preliminary words are in order about what we mean by ethnicity. We deliberately use the term "ethnicity," and not race, because we see it as a measure of individuals' cultural background rather than their biological ancestry. In keeping with other social scientists who study ethnicity, we use the term "ethnic group" to refer to a group of individuals who share certain fundamental patterns of culture, history, values, and beliefs.

In grouping youngsters by ethnicity, we employed a categorization scheme similar to that used by other social scientists, namely, one that asks individuals to classify themselves into one of seven categories: Asian, Black, Latino, non-Hispanic White, American Indian, Middle Eastern, or Pacific Islander (the specific instruction was "Select the one major ethnic group that best describes you"). We had insufficient numbers of students in our study from three categories (American Indian, Middle Eastern, and Pacific Islander) to draw statistically reliable conclusions about any of these ethnic groups, so in analyses designed with ethnic comparisons in mind, these youngsters were not included. Thus, when I write about ethnic differences or similarities in one or another aspect of adolescent development, I am referring to youngsters in one of four major ethnic groups: Black, Asian, Latino, or White. In analyses in which ethnicity was not a consideration— for example, if we simply wanted to examine the relation between school achievement and time spent in extracurricular activities—all of the students in our sample were included.

Any attempt to group individuals into categories defined by ethnic background is necessarily imperfect, even if individuals are classifying themselves. Any superordinate ethnic category necessarily mixes groups of individuals who come from various cultural backgrounds. The category we call "Asian," for example, combines individuals of Chinese, Japanese, Filipino, Korean, Southeast Asian, and South Asian descent—cultures that in numerous respects are quite diverse. Similarly, the category we call "Latino" is composed of students whose relatives come from Cuba, Puerto Rico, Central America, Mexico, and South America—again a rather varied group of backgrounds. The White youngsters in our sample generally were of European descent (in our study, "White" refers to non-Hispanic White youth), but this, of course, includes individuals from backgrounds as different from each other as Great Britain, Poland, and Greece.

We made the decision to use these broad categories knowing full well their limitations. But in our judgment, the alternatives—using more fine-grained categories or ignoring ethnicity entirely—were equally problematic. Further divisions of the groups into smaller categories (e.g., classifying youngsters in terms of their family's specific country of origin, or using concrete indicators such as fluency in one or another language, or adherence to certain cultural customs) is also imperfect, since even these categories frequently combine individuals from different cultural origins (e.g., rural versus urban Mexico, northern versus southern China, Protestant versus Catholic Irish, African individuals born in Africa versus African individuals born in America). Moreover, using a more fine-grained classification scheme would result in having very small numbers of individuals in any given category, rendering statistical analyses virtually impossible.

There are those who might argue that in light of these difficulties we should not have used ethnicity as a classifying variable at all. Indeed, had our study been conducted several decades earlier, when social scientists downplayed ethnicity in favor of socioeconomic status, we might not have studied ethnicity. Today, however, ethnicity is an exceedingly important variable in social science research as well as in public life generally. In contemporary America, ethnicity emerges as just as important a factor in defining and shaping individual experience as does social class or gender. Whether we like it or not, individuals use ethnicity in everyday life to classify themselves and others in an attempt to organize and understand their world. And, especially given the well-documented and widely reported findings concerning ethnic differences in achievement in this country, it would have been foolish, if not scientifically dishonest, to ignore this variable in our research.

This is not to say that we ignored other relevant information about individuals' ethnic background. Our surveys included detailed questions not only about the adolescent's self-categorization, but about the specific ethnic background of the adolescent's parents or stepparents, the family's immigration history, the languages spoken by the adolescent and the significant people in his or her life, and the adolescent's feelings and beliefs about his or her ethnic identity. These questions permitted us to perform more detailed analyses—examining, for example, how students whose families have recently come to the United States differ from youngsters of the same ethnic background, but whose families have been in America for several generations, or how different patterns of language use are related to school achievement among Latino or Asian youngsters.

Ultimately, the classification system we employed made the most sense in light of the particular research problem we were studying—adolescent achievement in American high schools in the late twentieth century. Dividing the world into the four-way scheme we ended up with—Asian, Black, Latino, and White—made sense, not only to us as researchers, but to the adolescents, their parents, and school personnel. A different research question, or one studied at a different time or in a different setting, might well have required a different basis for classification. In the final analysis, the utility of the categorization scheme we employed is borne out by the fact that it helps to account for differences in patterns of behavior. If the scheme were unreasonable, or foolhardy, or wrong, the findings it yielded would be less consistent and less interpretable.

WHY STUDY ETHNICITY?

One might think that studying ethnicity and achievement is the same as studying group differences in scholastic performance. Our investigation into ethnic differences in achievement was not primarily a documentation of differences in levels of achievement, however. The ethnic differences in achievement we found had been reported by numerous investigators long before we began our study. Our approach was aimed at understanding *why* such differences exist. What is it about Asian students that helps account for their above-average record? Why are Black and Latino students faring worse in school than their White or Asian peers? How can we account for individual students who are not performing as well as, or as poorly as, other members of their ethnic group? Are the factors that explain achievement similar or different as we move from one ethnic group to another?

The answers to these questions, it turns out, are far more complicated than the simple stereotypes that are so often (and often erroneously) casually exchanged. More important, in taking on these questions—questions about the underlying causes of ethnic differences in achievement—we were able not only to illuminate the issue of ethnicity and school performance, but to better understand the factors that affect *all* students' achievement. All of us, regardless of our personal background, have much to learn by examining why some groups are succeeding in school at far higher rates than others, and, as well, why some groups are performing so poorly.

Let me begin with a summary of what we found when we contrasted the school performance of students from different ethnic groups.

ETHNIC DIFFERENCES IN STUDENT ACHIEVEMENT
AND ENGAGEMENT

One of the most consistent observations reported by social scientists who study school achievement in this country is that Asian-American students perform, on average, substantially better than their White peers, who in turn outperform their Black and Latino counterparts. This finding has emerged over and over again, whether the index in question is based on school grades or performance on standardized tests of achievement. What is especially remarkable about the ethnic group comparisons of achievement is that they hold up even after taking into account other factors that might contribute to ethnic differences in performance, such as differences between ethnic groups in family income, household composition, or parental education.

We find precisely the same pattern of ethnic differences in our sample as other researchers have reported. That is, even when we compare students from identical social backgrounds, we still find that Asian students are outperforming their classmates who attend the very same schools, and that both Asian and White youngsters are achieving more than Black or Latino students. Although there are social class differences in school performance *within* every ethnic group—differences that favor, as one would expect, children from wealthier, more educated families—the differences *between* ethnic groups are not simply due to ethnic differences in income or parental education. That is, Asian students from low-income homes outperform comparably disadvantaged White, Black, and Latino students, and low-income White students score higher than comparably disadvantaged Black or Latino students; middle-class Asian students outperform middle-class Whites, who, in turn, outperform middle-class Black and Latino students; and so on. In other words, even though Black and Latino students are more likely to come from less advantaged backgrounds than White or Asian students, this difference in family resources does not fully explain the difference in the groups' school performance.

Nor can the difference be attributable to differences in the schools youngsters attend, since we find these ethnic differences even among youngsters enrolled in the very same schools. In fact, the relative standing of ethnic groups in their school performance was virtually identical across each of the nine schools we studied—in schools in both Wisconsin and California; in urban, suburban, and rural schools; in predominantly White and in predominantly minority schools. Across these very different settings, students of Asian descent were succeeding at a higher rate than all other students, and students of Black and Latino descent were achieving at a lower rate.

How large are the achievement differences we see when we compare ethnic groups, however? Whereas the average Asian students in our study were earning a mixture of A's and B's in school, other students were averaging grades of B's and C's, with White students earning more B's than C's, and Black and Latino students earning more C's than B's. Although these differences may not seem large at first glance, differences in grades of this magnitude clearly have genuine and important implications for how youngsters fare after completing high school. Put concretely, a student who graduates with a mixture of A's and B's on his or her transcript stands a much better chance of being admitted to a selective university than one with more C's than B's.

Group averages tell only part of the story. It is also important to look at the distribution of grades in each ethnic group, to get a sense of the range of student performance. After all, a group can end up with an overall average of C by having a high proportion of students earning C grades, or by having large numbers of students earning both A's and F's. How did the ethnic groups fare when we looked at their grades in this fashion?

White students' grades, in general, are tightly distributed around a B average, with two-thirds of the White students in our sample earning grades somewhere between B– and A–. What this means, therefore, is that relatively few White students are earning either very high *or* very low grades. Among Asian students, in contrast, close to 55 percent had grade-point averages of A or A–, compared with 35 percent of White students, 19 percent of Latino students, and 16 percent of Black students. At the other end of the spectrum, fewer than 10 percent of the Asian students had averages of C or lower, as opposed to 20 percent of the White students, 34 percent of Black students, and 38 percent of the Latino students.

We can look at this pattern in yet another way, by asking how the grades given out within a school are distributed across the ethnic groups. Here again we see the same basic pattern: Although Asian youngsters represented only 13 percent of our sample, they accounted for 27 percent of the students in our sample with straight-A averages, and 20 percent of the students with A– averages. Whites, who account for a little more than 60 percent of our sample, account for the same proportion of students with A or A– averages. In contrast, although Black and Latino students made up nearly one-fourth of our sample, they accounted for only 7 percent of the students with straight-A averages. Black and Latino students accounted for more than 40 percent of all the students in our sample with grade-point averages of C– or below.

These ethnic differences, as I mentioned earlier, were quite consistent within each of the different schools in our research, a finding that argues against the idea that the ethnic differences we observed are actually differences between schools or communities. If, for example, all of the Asian students were attending schools in which grading practices were liberal, and all of the Latino students were attending schools in which grading practices were more stringent, we could not tell if any observed ethnic difference in grades was really due to ethnicity or, instead, to the different schools' grading policies. For this reason, it was important to see if the ethnic differences in grades observed in the sample as a whole were also reported within each school. And they were.

Specifically, in every single high school community we studied, Asian students were earning a far higher proportion of the A's given out than would be expected by the sheer number of Asian students alone. In one school, for example, although Asian students accounted for only 8 percent of the student body, they accounted for nearly one-third of the students with straight-A averages! In contrast, Black and Latino students were always underrepresented among students with high averages, and always overrepresented among students with grades of C– or lower. White students were almost always clustered in the middle of the distribution, overrepresented among students earning B's, and underrepresented among those earning either very high or very low grades.

I noted earlier that the differences in school grades we observed among ethnic groups are large enough to make a difference in youngsters' future educational and occupational careers. We can also place ethnic differences in grades in perspective by comparing them to the differences we find when we contrast students regarding other demographic variables, such as gender, social class, household composition, or mother's employment status. For each of these demographic variables, we calculated the "net" effect of the variable in question after taking into account all of the other variables. Thus, we were able to estimate how much ethnicity "matters" after taking into account social class, household composition, gender, and maternal employment. Similarly, we were able to ask how much household composition matters after taking into account ethnicity, class, gender, and maternal employment, and so on.

As one would expect based on previous research, all of these factors are related to students' school performance. On average, girls earn higher grades than boys; youngsters from more affluent families earn higher grades than those from poorer households; students whose parents have never divorced earn higher grades than those who reside with a single parent or in a stepfamily; and students (especially boys) whose mother is employed full-time earn slightly lower grades than students with a mother who is not employed or works only part-time. Many of these findings have been reported by other investigators, and none of them is especially surprising.

Here's the big surprise, though: of all of the demographic factors we studied in relation to school performance, ethnicity is the most important. For example, even after we take into account the other demographic variables that make a difference, we find that the gap in grades between Asian students and Black or Latino students is nearly twice as big as the gap between students from the poorest families in our sample and those from the most affluent. Similarly, the gap between students from divorced and nondivorced homes is substantially smaller than the gap between the grades of White and Black or White and Latino students, and less than a third of the size of the gap between Asian and either Black or Latino students. In terms of school achievement, then, it is more advantageous to be Asian than to be wealthy, to have nondivorced parents, or to have a mother who is able to stay at home full-time.

Asian students are not merely distinguished from students of other backgrounds by their superior school grades and scores on standardized tests of achievement, however. Asian students also are significantly more engaged in school than their classmates—not really a surprise, since stronger engagement both leads to and results from higher grades.

Consider students' scores on some of the markers of engagement that we used in our study. Asian students spend more time on homework than other students. They cut classes less often, report higher levels of attention and concentration during class, and report less mind-wandering. They report being confused less often but challenged more often—a combination that certainly suggests emotional engagement in the classroom. On our measure of overall orientation toward school, which assesses how important a priority students think school is, Asian students outscore all other groups by a wide margin. In contrast, Black and Latino students spend significantly less time on homework than White or Asian students do, and this is not due to the fact that Black and Latino students are assigned less homework. Rather, Black and Latino students are more likely to report that they do not do all of the homework that they are assigned.

That we find ethnic differences in engagement, as well as in achievement, is extremely important. Some commentators have suggested that one reason for the greater success of Asian students, compared with White, Black, or Latino students, is their superior native intelligence. Our results suggest that this is unlikely. (Interestingly, other studies directly examining the genetic explanation have failed to support the view that Asian academic success is due to genetic advantages in intelligence.) A more reasonable reading of the evidence is that Asian students perform better in school because they work harder, try harder, and are more invested in achievement—the very same factors that contribute to school success among *all* ethnic groups. Indeed, as one of my colleagues once quipped, if Asian students were truly genetically superior to other students, they would not be spending twice as much time on homework each week as their peers in order to outperform them.

These strong and consistent ethnic differences in school achievement and engagement shed important light on the ongoing debate over school reform. One interpretation of our findings is that perhaps the school reform under consideration in some quarters is not the key. After all, the Asian students in our study were achieving high grades and maintaining strong engagement in the classroom despite the alleged deficiencies of their schools.

Similar conclusions have been reached in other studies. In one widely cited piece of research, the social scientists examined the achievement of Asian youngsters from Indochinese refugee families. These students came to the United States under enormously difficult conditions, with few economic resources and limited proficiency in English. All of the participants in the research went to school in poor, metropolitan areas—environments, as the researchers pointed out, that are hardly known for producing academic success. Indeed, these are the "disadvantaged urban schools" identified in so many reports as having the lowest levels of average student achievement in the country. Yet, despite all of these hardships, the Indochinese refugee children performed exceptionally well in school and on standardized tests of achievement, bettering in many cases their non-Asian counterparts for whom English was their native tongue. Whatever the faults of American schools—even those in the inner city—apparently some students are able to succeed in them. While this observation, of course, does not justify the continued existence of poor-quality schools, it does suggest that factors other than school quality must play an important role in determining student achievement.

EXPLAINING ETHNIC DIFFERENCES

To what can we attribute the relative superiority of Asian students in school and the relatively poor showing of Black and Latino students? As I have suggested, we cannot explain these differences away as an artifact of other differences in background, such as social class or household composition. And, because we find the same pattern of ethnic differences *within* schools as we do in the sample as a whole, we can be confident that the differences are not due to youngsters from different ethnic groups being enrolled in different schools. But what about discrimination within schools? Could it be the case that the lower grades of Black and Latino students are a product of teachers' discrimination, and that the higher grades of Asian students are due to teachers' favorable biases toward them?

Although many social critics believe that overt discrimination against Black and Latino students by teachers is rampant, the scientific evidence for this view is not strong. For example, studies show that the assignment of students to higher or lower tracks in high school is not heavily biased in terms of ethnicity, and track assignment is surely an instance where racial discrimination, if strong, would be manifested. Rather, research shows that students tend to be assigned to tracks on the basis of their past performance, and not their social background.

Nor do we see much evidence for the "prejudiced teachers hypothesis" in our own data. For instance, we asked students to report how often teachers at school were "unfair or negative" to them because of their ethnic background. In every ethnic group, reports of discrimination by teachers were rare. Although ethnic minority students in our study (and especially Black students) reported slightly more unfair or negative treatment by teachers than White students did, ethnic differences in levels of reported discrimination by teachers were much smaller than ethnic differences in achievement. Second, our analyses found that ethnic differences in school grades persist— and, in fact, are just as strong—after we take ethnic differences in perceived discrimination into account. In other words, whether we look separately at the group of students who report high levels of discrimination or separately at the group of students who report no discrimination, we see the same pattern of ethnic differences in school performance. Finally, and perhaps most significantly, Asian students and Latino students report identical levels of discrimination from teachers, even though the groups' grades are, as we have seen, quite far apart.

On the face of it, it would seem difficult to attribute ethnic differences in school performance to blatantly unfair or biased treatment by teachers. But there is a different version of the "discrimination hypothesis" that is frequently invoked, one concerning discrimination outside of school, in the broader society. Specifically, some writers have suggested that ethnic differences in school performance are due to differences in youngsters' perceptions of their chances for economic and occupational success as adults. This is one version of what has been called the "glass-ceiling hypothesis."

THE GLASS-CEILING HYPOTHESIS

I noted in the last chapter that one popular view is that school success is linked to students' perceptions about the likely economic rewards of academic accomplishment. An extension of this view is that ethnic differences in school achievement are due to ethnic differences in students' beliefs about the importance of doing well in school. One widely cited theory, for example, is that Black and Latino students do not achieve as much success in school as other students chiefly because they do not believe that academic success will have a significant payoff. According to this view, because Black and Latino students anticipate discrimination and prejudice in the labor force, they have little faith that scholastic success will actually lead to concrete economic rewards, and, as a consequence, they exert relatively less effort in school.

Is the higher level of achievement seen among Asian students, and the lower level of achievement seen among Black and Latino students, due to their having different beliefs about the payoff for academic success? That is, are Asian students more engaged in school because they are more likely than other students to have faith that doing well in school will pay off? Do Black and Latino students succeed less often because they do not share this belief?

The answer, interestingly enough, is no. When we examined students' responses on questions concerning the likely economic and occupational rewards of school success, we found no ethnic differences in how students answered these questions. In other words, Asian, Black, Latino, and White students are all equally likely to say that getting a good education (that is, going far enough in school) will have a genuine payoff down the road. And despite the popular belief that students have lost faith in the value of school to their futures, we found very few students—of any color—who do not believe that getting a good job is dependent on how many years of school one completes.

Where students did differ, however, was in their beliefs about the consequences of *failing* in school. We not only asked students if they thought that getting a good education would lead to a good job; we also asked if they thought that *not* getting a good education would hurt their chances in the labor force. It was in response to this latter question that we found the most striking ethnic differences.

By a substantial margin, Asian students were more likely than other students to believe that not doing well in school would have negative consequences for their future. In contrast, non-Asian students were less likely to hold this belief—they were far more cavalier about the potential negative effects of doing poorly in school. If anything, then, Asian students are successful not because of their stronger belief in the payoff for doing well, but because they have greater fear of the consequences of not doing well. It is undue optimism, not excessive pessimism, that may be holding Black and Latino students back in school. Their problem isn't that they have lost faith in the value of education; the problem is that many Black and Latino students don't really believe that doing poorly in school will hurt their chances for future success. The truth, of course, is that academic failure *does* affect the occupational and economic success of Black and Latino students, just as it does among their White and Asian peers.

BELIEFS ABOUT THE CAUSES OF SUCCESS AND FAILURE

Having students believe that it is worth investing time and energy in school is a necessary condition for academic achievement, but it is not sufficient by itself. In order to succeed, students also must believe that they have some control over how well they do in school, that their performance is somehow related to their effort, and that trying harder will lead to an improvement in their grades and test scores.

For some time now, psychologists have studied the ways in which we try to make sense out of what happens to us and, in particular, in the ways in which we explain our successes and failures. In the research literature, these explanations for success and failure are referred to as *achievement attributions*.

In our study, we carefully measured students' achievement attributions. We asked whether they believed the grades they received were due to personal factors (for instance, ability or effort) or to external factors (for example, the teacher's attitude, the difficulty of the material) and, as well, whether they attributed their performance to factors they had some control over (e.g., effort) versus those that they did not (e.g., luck). We asked these questions about both good and bad grades. Based on students' responses to these questions, we were able to classify them as having basically healthy or unhealthy attributional styles.

Students with healthy attributional styles believe that their performance in school is due to personal factors that are under their own control. They view success as the product of hard work, and failure as the result of insufficient effort. Although they are confident in their abilities, these students do not view their performance as fixed by their intelligence. More important, students with a healthy attributional style do not attribute their performance to external factors, such as how hard or easy the material is, whether their teachers like or dislike them, or whether they have good or bad luck.

At the other extreme are students with an unhealthy attributional style. These students downplay the role of effort in school success and failure. When they succeed, they view their accomplishment as the result of innate ability, an easy assignment, favorable treatment by teachers, or just plain good luck. When they fail, they attribute their performance to unfair teachers, bad luck, low innate ability, or having to confront an exceptionally difficult test, all factors over which they have no personal control.

Our studies, as well as a good deal of other research, clearly show that a student's attributional style is significantly predictive of his or her performance in school. Successful students, on average, are more likely to attribute their academic accomplishments to hard work and their occasional failures to a lack of effort. Unsuccessful students, in contrast, are more likely to see their performance as due to factors that are beyond their personal control.

What is especially interesting about our findings on achievement attributions, however, is the pattern of ethnic differences we observed. Asian students are significantly more likely than Black, Latino, or White students to have a healthy attributional style—that is, to see their success and failure as directly linked to how hard they work. Conversely, Asian students are less likely than other students to see success or failure as resulting from things outside their personal control, such as luck or the favoritism of teachers. This view—that effort is what really counts—is an important part of the belief system among youngsters (and adults) in Asian countries as well. Our study suggests that this cultural difference in beliefs is likely to be one reason for the superior showing of Asian students, both here and abroad.

The problem of unhealthy achievement attributions is pervasive within the United States. Compared with individuals from other cultures, Americans are far more likely to believe that success in school is dependent on native intelligence, that intelligence is fixed—either by genes or early experience—and that factors in the emotional and social realms play only an in-significant role in students' academic success. When we observe differences in students' test scores, we are likely to attribute both successes and failures to differences in students' talents, and we are likely to convey this message in the ways that we speak about success and failure in school (e.g., "You're just not good at science, honey"; "You've always been good at languages"; "You've done well in algebra because you're such a 'math whiz'").

These messages about the immutability of talent take hold in our chil-dren's minds at an early age. I saw this a few years ago in our son's account of why he received a B on a math test. To put this in proper perspective, Ben had just transferred to a new school that, unlike his old one, gave letter grades on students' exams and assignments. At his old school, his teachers had corrected students' homework and examinations, but had not graded them per se. Ben had been at his new school for about six weeks when he brought home a math test on which he had received a B.

I asked Ben if he knew why he had gotten the grade that he had received and, more important, if he knew what he could have done to have gotten a better grade. He looked at me, obviously upset at his performance and still trying to figure out how much his grades meant to his parents. "Suppose I'm just a B student?" he asked. "Then this is what I would expect to get."

I tried to explain to him that there was no such thing as a "B student"—that the grade he had received referred to his *exam*, not to him. But all the while I wondered how he could have so quickly transformed an evaluation of his work into a statement about his ability. Clearly, the message we give to students—you are what your grades say you are—is dangerously strong and salient, from a very early age.

Students, teachers, and parents in other parts of the world are far less likely than Americans to use the language of ability when discussing student performance. They are more likely to attribute differences in achievement to differences in students' motivation (how much they want to succeed), effort (how hard they exert themselves), or behavior (how much time they devote to their studies). Success, in their eyes, is not the outcome of inborn talent, but the product of systematic, motivated, hard work.

It is ironic that in the United States, a country that prides itself so much on its national "work ethic," we should place so little faith in hard work and so much in native ability. I suspect that one reason for the popularity of *The Bell Curve* is that its central premise—that intelligence, and therefore success, is fixed by genetic inheritance—is widely accepted as part of American folk "wisdom," even though the evidence for this belief is very weak. As you'll read later in this chapter, our findings concerning the drop in achievement that occurs as ethnic minority youngsters become acclimated to the American way of life indicates that school achievement is unlikely to be genetically determined.

THE MYTH OF ASIAN-AMERICAN MISERY

About ten years ago, *The New York Times* published an op-ed piece I wrote on the achievement gap between our students and Japan's. In that brief essay, I argued that the achievement gap was real, that it was indeed something to worry about, and that we had better address it. What were some of the "radical" suggestions I made? That American students spend more time on their studies and less time slinging hamburgers in fast-food restaurants, shopping, and partying with their friends; and that parents become more involved in their children's education. Shortly after the essay appeared, I heard from a tenth-grade social studies teacher from a school district in upstate New York. He had asked his students to read the essay and send me their responses.

The tenth-grade students' letters (which, incidentally, were written at about the sixth- or seventh-grade level) were uniformly critical of my piece. Yes, it is true, they wrote, that Japanese students outperform us in matters of achievement. But, they countered, how well rounded were those Japanese students? They might be *smarter*, one student wrote, but we're *happier*. And "everyone" knows about the high suicide rate among Japanese adolescents.

The notion that Asian students' academic success has taken a toll on their mental health and personal happiness is often used by American adolescents and parents to argue against steps we might take in this country to raise our own students' level of scholastic accomplishment. Yet it may come as a surprise to learn that the stereotype of the miserable Asian achiever is without foundation.

For example, contrary to popular belief and media hyperbole, the adolescent suicide rate today is higher in the United States than in Japan—and it has been higher for nearly twenty years. The notion that suicide is rampant among Japanese adolescents was valid forty years ago, but is no longer so today. The suicide rate among Japanese adolescents peaked in 1955 and has declined steadily since then. Among American adolescents, during this same time period, the suicide rate has more than *quadrupled*. Japanese adolescents may feel more pressure on them to do well in school than American adolescents, but this does not appear to have resulted in an increase in suicide.

The difference in mental health between Japanese and American adolescents, favoring Japanese youngsters, is also seen when less serious indicators of psychological disturbance than suicide are examined. A recent report from the University of Michigan cross-cultural study of achievement indicates, for example, that minor signs of psychological distress are also more common among American than among Japanese students. The researchers surveyed over one thousand students in each country and collected measures of stress, depression, anxiety, aggression, and somatic complaints (e.g., headaches, fatigue, sleep difficulties, gastrointestinal problems). Contrary to widespread belief, the American students reported *more* stress, *more* depression, *more* anxiety, *more* aggression, and *more* somatic complaints than did their Japanese counterparts.

Stereotypes to the contrary, it is simply not the case that Japanese students are made miserable by the more intense academic environment in which they grow up. Yet this same argument—that high achievement necessarily comes at a cost to one's mental health—has also surfaced in discussions about the achievement gap between Asian students and other students *within* the United States. The argument is familiar: Asian-American students may be achieving more, but they are paying a price with their mental health. Is there any truth to this assertion?

Because we collected extensive data on youngsters' mental health, we were able to compare Asian-American students with their peers on some of the same indices used by the Michigan researchers in their comparisons of American and Japanese students. Compared with their White counterparts, the Asian-American students in our sample reported significantly *less* psychological distress (depression and anxiety), *less* somatic distress (headaches, sleep problems, etc.), *less* delinquency (aggression, troubles with the law), and *less* drug and alcohol use than other students. A different set of researchers, studying junior high school students, reached the same conclusion: "Contrary to the common belief . . . Asian students' academic success [is] NOT at the expense of their social adjustment."

When we look a bit closer at the correlates of positive adolescent mental health—within *any* ethnic group—it is not difficult to see why Asian students report fewer psychological problems, "despite" their superior academic performance: in all ethnic groups, students who do well in school report better mental health and fewer behavioral problems than students who do poorly in school. In fact, academic success is one of the strongest predictors of psychological adjustment in childhood and adolescence.

This is not, as many individuals believe, because positive mental health facilitates academic success. This, interestingly, was the erroneous assumption behind the movement in some educational circles to raise youngsters' self-esteem—that is, it was wrongly believed that enhancing the way students feel about themselves would lead to improvements in their school performance. We now know that success in school leads to more positive self-esteem, not the other way around. Artificially inflating youngsters' feelings of competence does little to promote genuine achievement and probably impedes it, since it erodes youngsters' sense of standards. Paradoxically, if we are genuinely concerned about improving the mental health of American youth, we ought to take steps to see that they are genuinely challenged and achieve more in school.

THE HIGH COSTS OF AMERICANIZATION

Only a portion of the Asian and Latino youngsters currently attending school in the United States have parents who were born in this country. Any study of ethnic differences within the contemporary United States must therefore take into account the variation that exists both between and within different ethnic groups into which individual students and their parents were born. Because we collected data on youngsters' immigration histories, we were able to do this.

Most of us expect that individuals would have an especially tough time when they first arrive in a new country, and that, as a consequence, children who are recent immigrants would exhibit more distress and difficulty than their counterparts whose families have been living in the new country for some time. Given the fact that few nonnatives arrive in the United States fluent in English or acclimated to American customs and habits, one would expect that school would present a particularly demanding set of challenges for recent immigrants and their children. We would hypothesize, therefore, that students born outside the United States would be doing worse in school than those who are native Americans, and that native Americans whose families have been in this country for several generations would be faring better than their counterparts who arrived more recently.

Surprisingly, just the opposite is true: the longer a student's family has lived in this country, the worse the youngster's school performance and mental health. Consider some of the following findings from our study. Foreign-born students—who, incidentally, report significantly more discrimination than American-born youngsters and significantly more difficulty with the English language—nevertheless earn higher grades in school than their American-born counterparts. Although some commentators have speculated that the reason for this is economic—that families who are able to immigrate to the United States are from a higher social class than ethnic minority families who have been living here for several generations, and thus, more likely to succeed in school—our findings don't support this interpretation. The differences in school performance favoring immigrants over native Americans remain just as large even after we take family background into account.

It is not simply that immigrants are outperforming nonimmigrants on measures of school achievement. On virtually every factor we know to be *correlated* with school success, students who were not born in this country outscore those who were born here. And, when we look only at American-born students, we find that youngsters whose parents are foreign-born outscore those whose parents are native Americans.

The more Americanized students—those whose families have been living here longer—are less committed to doing well in school than their immigrant counterparts. Immigrants spend more time on homework, are more attentive in class, are more oriented to doing well in school, and are more likely to have friends who think academic achievement is important. Immigrants also are more likely to have the sort of healthy attributional style that is correlated with school success: in accounting for their scholastic successes and failures, they downplay the significance of luck, native ability, and other factors that are out of one's control; instead, immigrants see effort as the critical influence on achievement.

Differences between immigrants and nonimmigrants are also apparent when we look at various manifestations of mental health. Immigrant adolescents report less drug use, less delinquency, less misconduct in school, fewer psychosomatic problems, and less psychological distress than do American-born youngsters.

The adverse effects of Americanization are seen among Asian and Latino youngsters alike (that is, within each of the two largest populations of immigrant youth in this country), with achievement decreasing, and problems increasing, with each successive generation. Instead of finding what one might reasonably expect—that the longer a family has been in this country, the better their child will be faring in our schools—we find exactly the reverse. Our findings, as well as those from several other studies, suggest that becoming Americanized is detrimental to youngsters' achievement, and terrible for their overall mental health.

How can we account for this? One theory is that immigrant youngsters grow increasingly skeptical about the American system with each generation. Many Asian and Latino families arrive in the United States optimistic about their future and committed to the belief that the "land of opportunity" does in fact offer chances for economic and social advancement through schooling. Under these conditions, immigrant parents probably communicate to their children the need to work hard in school and instill in their youngsters a strong drive to achieve. Over time, however, youngsters discover that the actual opportunities are not as plentiful as they had been told, and that individuals of color often face prejudice and discrimination as they make their way through school and into the labor force. With each generation, therefore, ethnic minority youngsters become increasingly skeptical about the American dream and, consequently, increasingly disengaged from school.

An alternative explanation (although entirely consistent with the first) is that immigrant youngsters' values and attitudes about the relative importance of education are transformed as they become more and more Americanized. Since American adolescents do not typically value academic excellence, the more that immigrant youth acculturate to mainstream American values, the less they see school achievement as important. In other words, the declining achievement of immigrants with each successive generation is not the product of disenchantment in the face of limited opportunities, but a result of the *normative* socialization of ethnic minority youth into the mainstream's indifferent (or at least, ambivalent) stance toward school success. Because part of what it means to be an American teenager in contemporary society is adopting a cavalier attitude toward school, the process of Americanization leads toward more and more educational indifference.

Although we cannot settle this issue definitively with our data, it looks like the second explanation (the socialization of indifference) is more likely to be true than the first (the "dashed hopes" hypothesis). When we look at youngsters' beliefs about the importance of school success for their future occupational careers, we find no differences between recently arrived immigrants and first- or second-generation Americans. Nor do we find differences between these groups in their beliefs about the consequences of doing poorly in school. If the "dashed hopes" hypothesis were true, we ought to see it reflected in youngsters' answers to these questions about the importance of school (that is, recent immigrants should have more faith in the value of schooling than their native counterparts).

This is not the case, however. Instead, it looks as if the longer a family has lived here, the more its children resemble the "typical" American teenager, and part of this package of traits is, unfortunately, academic indifference, or even disengagement. Americanized ethnic minority youngsters—Asian and Latino alike—spend significantly more time hanging out with friends, more time partying, more time dating, more time on nonacademic extracurriculars, and more time with peers who value socializing over academics. In essence, the broader context of what it means to be an American teenager in the contemporary United States pulls students away from school and draws them toward more social and recreational pursuits.

Our findings on the costs of Americanization teach us a different, but equally important, lesson about genetic explanations of ethnic differences in achievement and school performance. If in fact the superior performance of

Asian students, or the poor performance of Latino students, were entirely due to genetic factors, we would not expect to find that student performance and behavior in school varied within these ethnic groups as a function of students' or parents' country of birth. The fact that students who have been brought up in the United States achieve less, are less interested in school, are more likely to engage in problem behavior, and are more interested in socializing than their nonnative counterparts from the same ethnic group points to a very strong environmental influence on achievement. It also says something very disturbing about the process of Americanization.

◈

SIX

The Power of Authoritative Parenting

It is tempting to lay the blame for the widespread disengagement of America's students on the school's doorstep—as the result of yet another deficiency in our teaching practices, curricula, or school policies that needs fixing. But the fact that many students, and many Asian-American students in particular, are able to become and remain engaged in the very same schools that are alleged to be in dire need of overhaul suggests that at least some of the roots of our achievement problem must reside outside our schools. Perhaps, instead of asking how schools should change in order to interest students who are presently disengaged, we might ask what it is about the students who *are* engaged in school that enables them to be this way.

More specifically, can we identify the factors in students' lives that encourage them to work hard, maintain high standards, worry about the consequences of failing in school, and accept personal responsibility for their successes and failures? What are the forces in students' lives that motivate them in school? And what are the forces that lead them to disengage?

Our research was the first large-scale study designed specifically to answer these questions. In the chapters that follow, as we search for the psychological and social origins of engagement and disengagement, we look at the main settings outside of school in which adolescents spend time. I begin with a source of influence most psychologists would agree is critically important to student success: the family.

THE FAMILY'S ROLE IN EDUCATION

From the child's earliest years, and continuing throughout elementary and secondary school, parents exert a profound and lasting effect on their children's achievement in school. They do this in at least three ways.

First, parents communicate specific messages to the child—both intentionally and inadvertently—about school and about learning. From these messages, children come to see whether school is important and, accordingly, how much effort they should expend there. Although most parents believe that the messages they convey on this subject are loud and clear, they are not always so. Indeed, in some households, children learn from their parents lessons about school that actually undermine their commitment to learning and achievement.

A second way in which parents influence their child's achievement is through their own behavior. Raising a school-aged child provides numerous opportunities for parents to demonstrate how committed they are to the process of education—with their actions, as well as with their words. Parents who can take advantage of these opportunities—by attending school functions, volunteering in school activities, helping with their child's course selection—let their children know that they value school. Through their behavior, they say that they are willing to match their child's devotion to school with a commensurate commitment of their own time and energy. Parents who are not able to take advantage of these opportunities, or, worse, who let these opportunities slip by, send a different message: that although we *say* that school is important, we don't have the time to get involved in it. In many such households, the child concludes that he or she doesn't have the time or energy to be very involved in school, either.

Perhaps the most important way that parents influence their child's achievement, however, is through the general atmosphere of the home environment—through what psychologists call their "style" of parenting. Even when parents are not intentionally attempting to shape their child's school career, they are doing so in their day-to-day approach to child-rearing, affecting their child's personality in ways that will manifest themselves in the classroom. Indeed, the way a child is treated in general—not just on specific school issues, but in general—affects the youngster's ability to become engaged in school. Some styles of parenting facilitate the development of a strong sense of engagement, whereas others do not. Some parenting styles actually interfere with healthy school engagement.

THE GAP BETWEEN PARENTS' INTENTIONS AND THEIR ACTIONS

Over the course of doing research on adolescent development for twenty years and giving dozens of lectures and workshops about adolescence to parents, I've had the opportunity to survey thousands of parents about their children's education. I can say with great certainty that the overwhelming majority of them desperately want their children to succeed in school. This is true of parents from all walks of life—from every ethnic group and social class, whether the parents are married or single, whether they live in cities, suburbs, or in rural areas. Indeed, the desire to have one's child succeed in school is one of the few common threads that unites almost all parents in this country.

Yet there is considerable slippage between this intention and the end result—so much slippage, in fact, that one must ask, "If so many parents really want their child to do well in school, why do only a minority of parents do what they ought to be doing?" The answer to this question is complicated, but our study provides a number of insights into the issue. Briefly, the reasons for the gap between parents' intentions and their actions fall into three categories: a lack of knowledge, a lack of skill, and a lack of opportunity.

A LACK OF KNOWLEDGE

By far the biggest reason for the failure of parents to translate their best intentions into the right behavior is a lack of knowledge. Many parents have the right goals for their children, but they simply do not know what works and what doesn't, or they have incorrect or misinformed ideas about what works, or they don't understand that there are effective and ineffective ways of accomplishing a particular goal in raising children. To be sure, one reason for this lack of knowledge is that those who study child development and child-rearing have not done as good a job as we should have in communicating to parents the results of our research—either we haven't bothered to disseminate these findings or we've done so in incomplete or inconsistent ways. One aim of this chapter is to lay out, in clear and coherent terms, what parents should consider doing in order to help their children grow up healthy and succeed in school.

But a second reason for the lack of knowledge stems from the erroneous belief held by many parents that effective child-rearing is either common sense (Everybody knows what good parents do—just ask any grandmother), instinctive (Some people are naturally good parents; either you are or you aren't, and it can't be taught), or relative (Who's to say what a good parent is, anyway?). These attitudes have long interfered with the best efforts of child development specialists to help parents see that effective parenting is more than just using common sense (or at least, that some people's common sense is just plain wrong); that parenting is a learned, not an inborn, skill; and that some approaches to child-rearing usually work better than others. Our study shows quite plainly that effective parenting is based on scientifically demonstrable principles, that these principles can be learned, and that following these principles generally works better than following other ones or adhering to none at all.

A LACK OF SKILL

One reason for the gap between parents' intentions and their actions, then, is a lack of knowledge. But there are a considerable number of parents who have the proper intentions and the correct knowledge, but who are not quite able to put this knowledge into practice. These parents may understand the general principles of effective parenting, but they may not know the concrete steps one must take to implement them—they have the knowledge but they lack the necessary skill. If you have ever tried to learn a new sport—tennis, golf, or skiing, for example—and have reached the point where you understood what to do but for some reason could not do it consistently, you know exactly what I mean. Many novice players, for example, intellectually grasp the mechanics of a tennis serve, a chip shot, or a stem Christie before they can actually serve accurately, hit the green consistently, or master a ski run. Similarly, many well-meaning parents intellectually grasp the "mechanics" of good parenting, but for some reason cannot actually do it.

In sports, this problem—knowing how to do something in theory but not in practice—is often solved through a process through which the complex motion is broken down into discrete steps, and the small steps are then learned through repetition. Mastering the component parts of a complicated athletic motion one at a time (in the tennis serve, for example, mastering the stance, the toss, the backswing, the swing, and the follow-through) is far more manageable than trying to learn the whole motion in one fell swoop. In much the same way, for parents who understand the principles of good parenting but are having trouble implementing them, effective parenting can be broken down into component parts and learned one component at a time. By repeating these components over and over, one can turn good parenting into a habit.

A LACK OF OPPORTUNITY

In a third category of less effective parents are those who know what to do and know how to do it, but who don't or can't practice effective parenting because other factors interfere. One of the challenges inherent in effective parenting is that it takes a good deal of time to be a good parent. For parents whose time or energy is limited—because of work commitments, marital stress, psychological problems, financial difficulty, or any number of reasons—good parenting is frustratingly out of reach, an ideal that is only an occasional possibility.

Unfortunately, there are few easy answers for parents in this situation. There are no tricks or shortcuts that provide a simple solution to the problem of too little time or divided energy. But the elements of effective parenting are the same in "nontraditional" as in "traditional" households—that is, they are the same for parents who work as for parents who are not employed, for single as for married parents, for poor as for middle-class parents. Parents living under occupational, marital, or financial stress may have to work harder to practice the principles of effective parenting, but it is critical for their child's welfare that they do. Children in nontraditional families benefit just as much from effective parenting as do children in traditional homes.

THE BEST HOME ATMOSPHERE FOR THE CHILD'S DEVELOPMENT

One of the oldest topics in research on child development is the study of different approaches to child-rearing and their effects on personality and cognitive development. Scientists interested in this subject have worked on this problem for at least sixty years, and there have been more published articles on the topic than on just about any other area in the field of child psychology.

After a great deal of systematic study, we now know that there are three fundamental dimensions of parenting that differentiate good parents from bad ones, and, accordingly, that differentiate the home environments of children who are successful in school from those who are not: *acceptance versus rejection*, *firmness versus leniency*, and *autonomy versus control*. Psychologists conceive of each of the three dimensions (acceptance, firmness, and autonomy) as a continuum along which parents vary (e.g., from extremely accepting to extremely rejecting, or from very firm to very lenient). Most parents fall somewhere between the two extremes of each range.

ACCEPTANCE

Acceptance refers to the degree to which the child feels loved, valued, and supported by his or her parents. Accepting parents are affectionate, liberal in their praise, involved in their child's life, and responsive to their child's emotional needs. Accordingly, children raised by accepting parents feel that they can turn to their parents when they have problems, that their parents encourage them, that their parents enjoy spending time with them, and that their parents are dependable sources of guidance or assistance.

At the other end of the acceptance continuum are parents who are cold—either actively rejecting, or passively aloof. These parents do not express much love for their child and are unresponsive to the child's emotional needs. They may have difficulty expressing affection because of their own upbringing, or they may believe that there is a danger in "spoiling" the child with too much love or nurturance. In either case, children whose parents are low in acceptance are likely to feel unloved, unsupported, and emotionally alone. They do not feel that their parents can be depended on, or that they can turn to them in times of difficulty.

FIRMNESS

The second dimension of parenting—firmness—refers to the degree and consistency of parental limits on the child's behavior. Parents who are high on this dimension have clearly articulated the rules that the child is expected to follow, and they make demands on the child to behave in a mature and responsible fashion. Children raised in this way know what their parents expect of them and know that there are consequences for violating their expectations.

Lenient parents, who have few rules or standards for their child's behavior, or who have rules but enforce them lackadaisically or inconsistently, fall at the other end of the firmness continuum. Some parents who are low in firmness are deliberately permissive, believing that excessive regulation by adults interferes with children's "natural" state. Other parents who are low in firmness are lenient not for philosophical reasons, but more from an inability to be firm and to exercise their authority. In either case, in the absence of sufficient control, children come to feel that "anything goes" or, alternatively, that it is impossible to know what is, or is not, acceptable behavior.

AUTONOMY

The third dimension, autonomy versus control, refers to how much parents tolerate and encourage their child's sense of individuality. Parents who are high in support for psychological autonomy solicit their child's opinions, encourage their child to express himself or herself, and, in adolescence, enjoy watching their child develop into a separate and autonomous individual. Children who grow up with parents who are high in autonomy support feel that self-expression is a valued trait, that their parents' love and respect for them is not contingent on their having the same opinions and ideas as their parents, and that it is important for a person to speak up for what he or she believes.

Parents who are high in control—low in their support for the child's autonomy—tend to value obedience over independence. They are likely to tell their children that young people should not question adults, that their opinions count less because they are children, and so on. Expressions of individuality are frowned upon in these families and are equated with signs of disrespect. Children who grow up under these circumstances come to feel that they should subordinate their own personality to the wishes of their parents.

HOW CHILDREN ARE AFFECTED BY ACCEPTANCE, FIRMNESS, AND AUTONOMY SUPPORT

Since the late 1950s, literally hundreds of studies have been conducted that examine acceptance, firmness, and autonomy support and their consequences for the child's development. The gist of these studies has been remarkably consistent: children develop in more healthy ways when their parents are relatively more accepting, relatively firmer, and relatively more supportive of the child's developing sense of autonomy.

Although fads in child-rearing advice have come and gone over the years (and more fads are sure to follow), no scientific studies have challenged these basic findings. If parents understand and accept this, they are on the way toward becoming more effective parents and helping their child develop in healthy ways.

The consistency with which findings on the benefits to children of acceptance, firmness, and autonomy support have appeared in research studies is really quite remarkable, especially since scientists have used all sorts of methods and sources of information. More important, the consistency of this research argues against the widely held notion that good parenting is all relative. In the past four decades of concerted, scientific study, no research has ever suggested that children fare better when their parents are aloof than when they are accepting, when their parents are lenient rather than firm, or when their parents are psychologically controlling rather than supportive of their psychological autonomy. Indeed, in an era in which scientific "facts" about diet, exercise, and lifestyle seem to change almost monthly (Should you eat oat bran? Drink red wine? Exercise gently or intensively?), the consistency of research on effective parenting is impressive.

During the past fifteen years, researchers even have been able to identify with some precision the *specific ways* in which acceptance, firmness, and autonomy support contribute to the healthy development of the child. Each aspect of effective parenting matters, but each matters for slightly different outcomes.

Acceptance seems to matter most for children's overall adjustment and sense of self-worth; because they feel loved, they feel lovable. As a result, children who feel valued and supported by their parents have higher self-esteem, more positive self-conceptions, and a happier, more enthusiastic outlook on life. Not surprisingly, they are more sociable and more socially skilled—for instance, at younger ages they play more cooperatively with other children, and when they are older, they are more popular and socially confident.

Firmness matters more for children's sense of self-control. Children whose parents have been consistently firm are better able than other youngsters to control their impulses and abide by rules set down by others. When they are younger, they have fewer problems with aggression, fighting, and what is sometimes called "acting out," and they have fewer disciplinary and conduct problems when they are older. Presumably, children with relatively more strict parents have learned from an early age that there are limits on how one behaves, and over time they have incorporated their parents' standards and expectations and made them their own. With time, regulation by the parent becomes self-regulation, the most effective method of control.

The beneficial effects of support for the child's psychological autonomy are seen most clearly in the realms of competence and responsibility. Children whose parents have granted them sufficient psychological autonomy are more self-reliant, more industrious, and more competent than other children. They have a stronger sense of their own abilities, and they are more persistent and determined when challenged in school or in some other achievement situation. Because they are more likely to feel confident, and less likely to feel helpless, children raised with sufficient autonomy support are less susceptible to feelings of depression or anxiety.

Through what processes are these parenting practices transformed into healthy psychological outcomes in the child? In each case—acceptance, firmness, and autonomy support—the message communicated by the parent to the child becomes incorporated into the child's self-conception—in psychological jargon, a process called "internalization." In essence, the parent's love for the child, expressed through acceptance, nurturance, and affection, becomes self-love, or, as it is more commonly called, self-esteem. In a similar vein, the parent's emphasis on control is internalized by the child and evolves into self-control. And the parent's view of the child as an autonomous individual capable of independence is transformed into the child's view of himself or herself as a competent, separate, responsible person.

THE SUM IS GREATER THAN THE PARTS

During the 1960s and 1970s, child psychologists discovered two very interesting things about these three essential elements of effective parenting. First, it was found that acceptance, firmness, and autonomy had different effects on the child when they occurred together (for example, when a child's parents were accepting *and* firm *and* supportive of autonomy) than they did when they were experienced separately (for example, when a child's parents were accepting but not firm, or firm but not supportive of autonomy). In particular, the effects of any one of the three elements of effective parenting were amplified when it occurred in conjunction with the other two. In other words, although all children benefit from having parents who are accepting, children with accepting parents who are also firm and supportive of the child's autonomy profit more from their parents' acceptance than do children whose parents are equally accepting, but permissive or psychologically restrictive. The same general pattern holds true for firmness and autonomy support: these qualities in a parent have stronger effects on the child when they are accompanied by each other and by sufficient levels of parental acceptance.

Acceptance is especially critical for the child to be able to reap the benefits of parental firmness, a point to be stressed. Many parents understand the need to be firm, to have standards for their child's behavior, to be good disciplinarians. But research shows that in order for discipline to be effective, children need to feel that their parents are loving and nurturing as well. In the absence of acceptance, parental firmness may seem to the child to be harsh, unfair, and overly punitive, and these feelings may provoke noncompliance or even outright defiance. Children, as a rule, are far more likely to do what their parents tell them when they feel that their parents love them and have their best interests at heart. When children do not sense this—as is often the case in homes where parents are aloof or rejecting—they are less responsive to their parents' attempts at discipline. Thus, while it is true that "love is not enough," discipline is not enough, either.

PARENTING STYLES

A second intriguing finding to appear in studies of child-rearing conducted during the late 1960s and early 1970s was that parents' scores on measures of acceptance, firmness, and autonomy support were typically patterned in meaningful ways. One commonly observed group of parents, for example, were those who were low in acceptance, high in firmness, and low in autonomy support. Another group was composed of parents who scored high on acceptance, low on firmness, and high on autonomy support. Psychologists began to look at these patterns more closely in order to identify their underlying causes, predominant features, and associated outcomes in the child. These patterns have come to be known as parenting "styles," because they reflect overall approaches to child-rearing—styles of parenting—rather than situation-specific parenting practices.

We might think of the difference between general parenting style and specific parenting practices in the same way that we think of the difference between someone's general style of dressing and the specific clothes he or she put on this morning. Just as, say, a generally conservative dresser will own many different outfits that share in common some basic features (restrained colors, highly tailored lines, understated patterns), a parent with a certain style of parenting will engage in somewhat different parenting practices from time to time, but the practices will share some fundamental, underlying characteristics. And just as you can look in someone's closet and draw inferences about that person's style of dress by drawing generalizations about the specific elements of clothing you see, psychologists can look at a parent's overall pattern of parenting and draw inferences about his or her style.

Although in theory one could imagine a large number of different parenting styles, based on all sorts of different combinations of acceptance, firmness, and autonomy support, in reality this is not the case. Basically, three styles of parenting have emerged over and over again across a number of studies, and if you think of the families with whom you are acquainted (including your own), you can probably think of examples of each.

One group is composed of relatively harsh, firm, and psychologically controlling parents; they have been dubbed "authoritarian" or "autocratic." Authoritarian parents have adopted a sort of "Do it because I say so" attitude toward their child, and they discipline by asserting their power and control, often in cold and punitive ways. Authoritarian parents are frequently rigid in their approach to child-rearing, preferring consistency (even when they know they're wrong) to compromise or flexibility.

A second commonly observed cluster of parents are accepting, exceedingly lenient, and supportive of their child's psychological autonomy. This style has been labeled "permissive," or "indulgent," because parents who adopt this approach permit their children to have their way and tend to indulge their children's wishes. Permissive parents adopt a laissez-faire attitude toward raising children, typically striving to keep their child "happy" by avoiding setting limits and engaging in conflicts with the child over his or her behavior.

A third cluster of parents found in most studies is high in acceptance, firmness, and autonomy support. This style of parenting has come to be known as "authoritative" or "responsive" parenting. Unlike permissive parents, authoritative parents do not hesitate to set limits on their child's behavior or maintain standards for the child to live up to. And unlike authoritarian parents, who also have limits and standards for the child, authoritative parents discipline from a position of acceptance rather than power, and they do so in ways that encourage, rather than squelch, the child's growing sense of autonomy. In other words, authoritative parents are firm without being harsh, strict without being psychologically stifling.

These three different approaches to parenting reflect in part very different child-rearing values and different beliefs about what is best for the child. Autocratic parents view their main responsibility as controlling the child's impulses. They believe that the most important thing their child can learn is to obey and respect authority, and they worry that too much affection will interfere with this learning process. Although they may appear to be aloof or cold (either to an outside observer or to the child), it is not because they don't care about the child, but because they worry that too much acceptance—a "spare the rod, spoil the child" mentality—will get in the way of the more important business of teaching obedience.

Permissive parents approach child-rearing from a completely different perspective. They view their main responsibility as making sure that their child is happy and that his or her needs are gratified. Unlike authoritarian parents, who worry that without appropriate controls, children's "bad" qualities will overwhelm their good ones, permissive parents believe that children are basically good, and that parents should support children in their natural inclinations. Permissive parents are not there to control the child, but to facilitate growth by staying out of the way as much as possible. In fact, these parents worry about the risk of excessive control—that the child's creativity, curiosity, and inquisitiveness will be stifled by too much emphasis on authority. They acknowledge that children can make bad choices, but they believe that the beneficial learning that takes place as a result of making mistakes outweighs the negative consequences of these errors.

Authoritative parents have a different view of their responsibility. If authoritarian parents place a premium on obedience, and permissive ones on happiness, authoritative parents emphasize self-direction. They see their role as helping their child learn how to become responsible—both in the sense of being self-reliant (personally responsible), but also in the sense of being able to function as a member of a group (socially responsible). To authoritative parents, the primary issue isn't whether a child is obedient or happy, but whether the child is mature. And in their view, maturity is fostered by guiding the child toward proper behaviors and nurturing the child's developing sense of judgment.

I can illustrate these differences among parenting styles by describing how different parents might approach the same situation: reacting to a teenager who one night has come home after his or her curfew. An autocratic parent, who places an emphasis on obedience, would probably punish the adolescent for disobeying or disregarding the curfew. A permissive parent, concerned about the child's happiness, would likely ignore the infraction or treat it lightly, for fear of upsetting the child or disturbing the family peace. An authoritative parent, stressing maturity, would find out why the teenager was late, discuss the legitimacy of the reason, and help the teenager see why a responsible person would have called home before coming back late—regardless of the reason.

Each of these goals—obedience, happiness, and maturity—is laudable, and all three are desired to one extent or another by almost all parents. If given the choice, very few parents would say they don't care whether their child is obedient, happy, or mature, and fewer still would say they value disobedience, unhappiness, or immaturity. Indeed, the question isn't really whether a parent values one of these traits rather than the others, but where the general emphasis in the household is put. In assessing a parent's style, then, it is important to ask how the parent behaves when there is a potential for conflict between two or more of these goals. When forced to choose among various responses in disciplinary situations, authoritarian parents will more often emphasize obedience and compliance; permissive parents, happiness and gratification; and authoritative parents, maturity and responsibility.

AUTHORITATIVE PARENTING AND CHILD DEVELOPMENT

For most of the last twenty years, the notion that authoritative parenting is superior to other styles of parenting has enjoyed increasingly widespread acceptance among social scientists who study child-rearing and its effects, and for good reason. Virtually without exception, research has indicated that authoritatively raised youngsters reap the combined benefits of growing up under conditions of acceptance, firmness, and autonomy support. Compared with their peers who have been raised in authoritarian or permissive homes, youngsters who come from authoritative households are more self-reliant, more cheerful, more socially skilled, more curious, and more self-controlled than other children throughout the preschool and elementary school years.

Although support for the benefits of authoritative parenting has appeared consistently in the scientific literature on parent-child relations, this uniformity has not been mirrored in the advice books and videos more readily available to parents themselves. While it is true that it takes a certain degree of time for all scientific findings to make their way from the professional literature into more popular outlets, surely forty years of consistent research findings ought to be enough to generate consistent products for general consumption. There are, thankfully, many excellent books for parents that accurately reflect the scientific research base. But there are far too many on the market that do not, and there are some publications that are truly appalling in how far they diverge from what rigorous, systematic studies of child-rearing clearly recommend.

IS CONSISTENCY BETWEEN PARENTS ESSENTIAL?

When I lecture on child-rearing to college students enrolled in courses in child psychology or give a talk to a group of parents, someone invariably asks about the situation of the child who has one parent of one type and a second parent of another. Suppose one parent is permissive, for example, and the other is authoritarian. Is this confusing to the child? Is one style inherently more powerful than another? Are children more affected by their mother or by their father?

All of these questions are interesting in theory, but it turns out that they are far less interesting in practice. In the overwhelming majority of families with adolescents—about 75 to 80 percent— mothers and fathers follow the same basic approach to parenting, so the chances of a child being exposed to great inconsistency are much smaller than one might think.

There are three reasons for this. First, because people tend to marry individuals from a similar background and with similar values, husbands and wives tend to be somewhat in agreement about many of the essential elements of child-rearing before they even have children. Second, because mothers and fathers influence each other over time, by the time the child has reached adolescence the two parents' styles will have drifted together, typically because one parent's style sets the tone for the other's. Finally, and sadly, many couples who have deep and fundamental disagreements about how to raise children often disagree on so many other issues as well that they stand a good chance of divorcing before the child reaches adolescence.

For all of these reasons, it is extremely rare for a teenager to encounter markedly different parenting from his or her mother and father. Because we had such a large sample of families in our research, we were able to look more closely at the small group of children who find themselves in this situation. In general, among adolescents living with both mother and father, those with one authoritative parent fared better than those with no authoritative parent, even if the two nonauthoritative parents were consistent in their parenting style. In other words, consistency per se is less important than having at least one authoritative parent in the home.

CHARACTERISTICS OF ADOLESCENTS FROM DIFFERENT TYPES OF HOMES

Most of the research that had been done before our study documented the positive consequences of the three elements of good parenting for children in the preschool and elementary school years, but stopped short of saying that these advantages continued once the child had entered adolescence. In our study, we were able to examine whether the benefits of acceptance, firmness, and autonomy support continued into the high school years.

Using measures of acceptance, firmness, and autonomy support, we attempted to classify the families in our sample into the authoritarian, permissive, and authoritative clusters that had been identified in previous research. We then looked specifically at four sets of outcomes: how the youngsters were developing psychologically, especially in such areas as self-reliance, self-esteem, and social competence; how well the youngsters were doing in staying out of trouble—away from drugs, alcohol, delinquency, and misconduct in school; whether the youngsters reported any signs of psychological distress, such as anxiety or depression; and, of course, how engaged and successful the youngsters were in school.

For the most part, we found that the same sorts of differences observed among younger children from authoritative, authoritarian, and permissive homes also were found among adolescents. Specifically, teenagers who had been raised in authoritative homes—homes in which parents are accepting, firm, and supportive of their child's psychological autonomy—fare significantly better than their peers from other types of households. Psychologically, authoritatively reared adolescents are more confident, more poised, more persistent, more self-reliant, and more responsible. They are less likely to use or abuse drugs or alcohol, and less likely to be involved in delinquency or in more minor forms of misbehavior, such as cheating on school tests or cutting classes. Adolescents from authoritative homes report less anxiety, less depression, and fewer psychosomatic problems, such as insomnia or problems controlling their appetite. And, not surprisingly, adolescents from authoritative homes do best in school, as measured by their grades, their attitudes toward schoolwork, and the time they invest in their studies.

Teenagers from authoritarian homes have a psychological profile that suggests that they have been overpowered into obedience. When it comes to things like misbehavior, teenagers from authoritarian homes look just as good as their peers from authoritative homes: they are less likely than other youngsters to use drugs and alcohol and less likely to get into other types of trouble as well. But when it comes to measures of psychological well-being, the disadvantages associated with authoritarian rearing are readily apparent. Teenagers from authoritarian home environments have lower self-esteem than other youngsters, and are less self-reliant, less persistent, and less socially poised. Although the grades they earn in school are nearly as good as those of teenagers from authoritative homes, teenagers from authoritarian homes have significantly worse views of their own competencies and abilities. In sum, authoritarian parenting seems to make adolescents toe the line, but it does not help them become more self-assured or psychologically mature. Given the emphasis placed on obedience and compliance in these households, these results are not surprising.

Adolescents from permissive homes are in some ways a mirror image of those from authoritarian homes. On measures of misbehavior and lack of compliance with adult authority, permissively raised adolescents often appear to be in some trouble. Their drug and alcohol use is higher than other adolescents, their school performance is lower, and their orientation toward school is weaker. All of this suggests some reluctance, or perhaps difficulty, in buying into the values and norms of adults (most of whom would counsel staying out of trouble and doing well in school). At the same time, though, the adolescents from permissive homes report a level of self-assurance, confidence, and social poise comparable to that seen in the teenagers from authoritative households. Especially attuned to their peers, adolescents from permissive homes are both more capable in social situations with their age mates and more susceptible to their friends' influence. All in all, it appears as if parental permissiveness leads teenagers to be relatively more oriented toward their peers, and less oriented toward their parents and other adults, such as teachers.

The differences we observed among adolescents from authoritative, authoritarian, and permissive homes point once again to the power of authoritative parenting—this time, during adolescence—as an approach to child-rearing that protects adolescents from getting into trouble while at the same time promoting their maturity and successful school performance.

DISENGAGED PARENTS

For the overwhelming majority of the families in our study—about 70 percent—one of the three main parenting styles aptly described the global atmosphere of the home environment. However, a significant minority of families in our study could not be categorized as authoritative, authoritarian, or permissive. Many of these parents combined the "worst of both worlds," sharing emotional aloofness with the authoritarian families and disciplinary leniency with permissive ones. These parents seemed remarkably uninvolved in their children's lives—either as sources of social support or as providers of guidance or structure. We termed these parents "disengaged."

Disengaged parents have, for one reason or another, "checked out" of child-rearing. They have disengaged from responsibilities of parental discipline—they do not know how their child is doing in school, have no idea who their child's friends are, and are not aware of how their child spends his or her free time—but they have also disengaged from being accepting and supportive as well. They rarely spend time in activities with their child, and seldom just talk with their adolescent about the day's events.

It is hard to estimate the number of truly disengaged parents, but it appears to be somewhere around 25 percent, depending on the specific index we use. In our study, we asked many questions aimed at assessing how involved parents were in various aspects of their child's life, both inside and outside of school. We found that about one-fourth of students are allowed to decide what classes to take in school without discussing the decision with their parents, that about 30 percent of parents did not know how their child was doing in school, and that one-third of parents did not know how their child spends his or her spare time. And parental disengagement is not just limited to their youngsters' school lives: one-fourth of the students we surveyed said their family "never" did anything together for fun, and only 30 percent said their parents spend some time talking with them each day.

Our estimate of the prevalence of parental disengagement at around 25 percent is in accord with data reported in a 1994 survey conducted for the Metropolitan Life Insurance Company by the Lou Harris survey firm. In that study, for example, 22 percent of high school students said they never talked to their parents about problems they were having with other students, and 25 percent of students surveyed said they wondered if their parents really loved them. Between one-fourth and one-third of the students surveyed said that they wished their parents were more involved in their schoolwork.

In all likelihood, then, about one in four American high school students has parents who are disengaged from his or her life in one or more important ways. Because this estimate comes from surveys of students who are present in school, however, it is likely to underestimate the overall proportion of households with disengaged parents, since students who are frequently absent from school, or who have dropped out of school, are more likely to come from disengaged homes than students who stay in school through graduation. If we were to factor into the equation the appreciably higher level of parental disengagement among the families of the sizable minority of adolescents who miss school regularly or who have left school before graduating, the estimate of parental disengagement in the population overall would probably be closer to 30 percent, and perhaps even as high as one in three.

The view that a substantial minority of contemporary American parents are disengaged from parenting is shared by parents themselves. The MetLife survey cited above also asked parents to evaluate the parenting of their peers—that is, to estimate how many parents in their communities were meeting their responsibilities. Interestingly, parents' judgment about the behavior of other parents paints a picture that is even more worrisome than that obtained from surveys of children. Half the parents queried in the

MetLife study thought that the majority of other parents left their children alone too much after school, took too little interest in their children's education, failed to motivate their children to do well in school, and failed to discipline their children adequately. Parents' estimates are not as reliable as systematic surveys, but they do give us some idea of what people believe is taking place in their communities and neighborhoods. The picture is not a pretty one.

THE COSTS OF PARENTAL DISENGAGEMENT

The differences we observed among the adolescents from authoritative, authoritarian, and permissive upbringings, while significant, were far smaller in magnitude than the differences between these youngsters, considered as a group, and the adolescents from disengaged homes. That is, although it is relatively better for a child to be raised by authoritative parents than by authoritarian or permissive ones, it is far worse to grow up with disengaged parents. Whatever their shortcomings, permissive or authoritarian parents are at least engaged in the business of parenting.

The problems associated with disengaged parenting were evident across all of the domains we studied. Adolescents from disengaged homes were substantially more likely to show psychological immaturity and adjustment difficulties, as evidenced by less self-reliance, lower self-esteem, and diminished social competence. Adolescents from these sorts of homes were more likely to show psychological problems, both in terms of various types of misconduct (drug use, delinquency, etc.) and in terms of various types of distress (anxiety, depression, psychosomatic complaints). And adolescents from disengaged homes were less interested in and less successful in school, as indexed by any number of measures of engagement or academic performance. When we followed these youngsters over time, we found that their problems increased substantially over the course of high school, so that the adjustment gap between adolescents from engaged versus disengaged homes became wider and wider with time.

When viewed alongside the figures we cited earlier, on the high prevalence of parental disengagement, our findings concerning the problems associated with disengagement point to real problems for our society. Parental engagement in their children's lives is one of the most important—if not the single most important—contributors to healthy psychological development. Not only our studies, but those of several other researchers, show quite clearly that adolescents whose parents are not sufficiently engaged in their lives are more likely to get into trouble than are other youngsters. Parental disengagement is a very good predictor of many of the problem behaviors whose levels have reached alarming proportions: alcohol and drug abuse, delinquency and violence, suicide, and sexual precocity. And, as we have seen, parental disengagement is also a very good predictor of academic difficulties and low school achievement. Compared with students whose parents are involved in their schooling, youngsters with relatively more disengaged parents earn lower grades in school, are less committed to school, and are less motivated to do well in the classroom. That nearly one in three parents is disengaged from their adolescent's life is clear reason to worry about the future well-being of America's young people.

SEVEN

The Home Environment of Academically Successful Students

Because we were especially interested in the role of the family in promoting or hindering success in school, we devoted considerable effort to understanding the psychological mechanisms through which parenting practices affect school achievement. When we learned that adolescents from authoritative homes—homes in which parents are warm, firm, and supportive of the adolescent's developing sense of autonomy—perform better in school than their peers, we turned our attention to investigating what it was in particular about growing up in an authoritative environment that facilitates success in school.

In an earlier chapter, I discussed how students' engagement in school—their motives, values, beliefs, and behaviors—affects their academic performance. By linking this information about student engagement and its important role in achievement with what we know about effective parenting and adolescent development, we are able to explain at least part of the connection between what goes on at home and what takes place in school. Simply put, authoritative parenting contributes to the development of the motives, values, beliefs, and behaviors that make students interested in school, and this commitment permits children to achieve more academically. Nonauthoritative parenting, in contrast, undermines these attributes and promotes the development of an orientation toward learning that interferes with school success.

The benefits of growing up in an authoritative household are reflected in youngsters' school performance as early as the middle elementary school years. But if we track students' engagement in school over the course of high school, we find that the gap between children from authoritative and nonauthoritative homes actually widens over time. The students with authoritative parents improve relatively more each year than other students, while the students with disengaged parents fall further and further behind. In any given year, the gap grows by only a small amount, but when this difference accumulates over the course of secondary school, the aggregate impact on a youngster's school record is considerable.

Parents do, therefore, make a difference in their children's school performance. Where does intelligence, or ability, fit into this picture? As I've pointed out, a student's performance in school is influenced by his or her ability, but it is only *influenced* by it, not *determined* by it. (We might think of ability as setting an upper limit on a student's actual performance.) There are many students with high ability who do not perform as well as we would otherwise anticipate—so-called "underachievers." What authoritative parenting does is to help close the gap between a student's ability and his or her actual achievement—that is, to minimize "underachievement"—by helping the student to become sufficiently engaged in school to profit from the experiences encountered there.

HOW AUTHORITATIVE PARENTING WORKS

Our research pointed to two specific psychological advantages that authoritatively reared children have over their peers when it comes to school engagement. First, growing up in an authoritative home makes youngsters more psychologically mature, especially when it comes to their willingness to work hard and to take pleasure in doing something well. As I noted earlier, adolescents from authoritative homes are more self-reliant, more persistent, and more responsible than their classmates. This more mature psychological makeup equips authoritatively reared students to do better in school, especially as they move into high school, where students are expected to be more self-directed and to take more responsibility for their own work. In this regard, children from authoritative homes are psychologically more primed for school success.

A second psychological benefit of authoritative parenting is seen in the ways that children from different types of homes explain their academic successes and failures. Authoritatively raised children are more likely to have the healthy attributional style that is such an important part of being engaged in school. They tend to attribute their success to hard work and, when they are not successful, they see their failure as due to lack of effort. When things go well in school, they see their success as resulting from their own diligence; when things go poorly, they believe the cause was their not working hard enough. As a result, when children from authoritative homes face a challenge in school, they feel more confident that they—not their teachers, their genes, or the luck of the draw—control their scholastic fate. Students from homes with other parenting styles, in contrast, often attribute success or failure to conditions that they have little control over, like ability or luck. As a result, when challenged, they are more nervous about the outcome. And, when given the choice between a challenging course and an easy one, or a difficult assignment and a less demanding one, children from nonauthoritative homes are more likely to take the easy way out.

PARENTAL INVOLVEMENT IN SCHOOL

One way that authoritative parenting works, then, is by enhancing the student's general psychological state. A second contribution of authoritative parenting is related to the parents' own behavior, and, more specifically, with their relationship to the school as an institution. Authoritative parents have many of the same psychological characteristics that their children have. Like the products of their own child-rearing, authoritative parents tend to be persistent, self-reliant, and conscientious. Not surprisingly, these parents are more involved in their youngsters' schooling than other parents are.

In recent years, we have all heard so much about the importance of parents' involvement in their children's education that it has become a bit of a cliché. But like all clichés, there are elements of truth to this one. All other things being equal, children whose parents are involved in school do better than their peers.

Because we studied children and their parents over time, we were able to separate out cause and effect in looking at parental involvement and school performance. This was important to do, because it is very likely that, when students do well in school, this inspires their parents to become more involved in their child's education. But while this turns out to be correct, the reverse is also true: being an involved parent actually *leads to* student success. For example, if we saw two students with equal grades in school at one time and followed them over the course of the next year, we would find that the student whose parents were more involved in his or her education would earn better grades over time than the student whose parents were less involved.

As a general principle, then, parental involvement works. The problem for schools and parents, however, is that there are many different ways for parents to be involved in their children's education, and it has been hard to figure out which types of involvement work best. In our study, we looked very carefully at this question in order to be as specific as possible about the advice we can give to parents and educators.

Our findings were somewhat surprising. The type of parental involvement that matters most is not the type of involvement that parents practice most often—checking over homework, encouraging children to do better, and overseeing the child's academic program from home. These behaviors do not harm children's performance in school, but by themselves they make surprisingly little, if any, positive difference in student performance, especially once a child has reached high school. These behaviors may play a role in stimulating achievement during elementary school, but we don't find much evidence of their usefulness once a child has entered secondary school.

What sort of parental involvement is worthwhile? Our research shows that the type of involvement that makes a real difference is the type that actually draws the parent into the school physically—attending school programs, extracurricular activities, teacher conferences, and "back to school" nights. These sorts of activities make a small but significant difference in student achievement. It is not simply that having a successful student leads parents to become more involved; parental involvement of this sort boosts their students' performance in school.

Why should the second type of parental involvement have the greater effect? The answer, I think, has to do with the sorts of messages each type of involvement communicates, not only at home, but at the school itself. Showing up at school programs on a regular basis takes a great deal more effort than helping out at home, and this effort does not go unnoticed by students or by school personnel. When parents take the time to attend a school function—time off from an evening activity or time off from their own jobs—they send a strong message about how important school is to them, and, by extension, how important it should be to their child. When this sort of involvement occurs regularly, it reinforces the view in the child's mind that school and home are connected, and that school is an integral part of the whole family's life.

Attending school functions may be even more important for the message it communicates to teachers and other school personnel. Teachers cannot help but pay closer attention to students whose parents they encounter frequently at school programs, for both positive and negative reasons. On the positive side, the added attention stems from a sort of halo effect—Susie's parents are interested in her education, so Susie must be, too. But the attention also stems from the teacher's knowledge that Susie's parents are the sort of parents who are more likely to take action if something in Susie's education is not going right. A teacher knows that an involved parent is going to be the first one calling the principal's office if his or her child has not been treated properly in class. And if a parent wants a teacher to know that he or she is involved, there is no better way than showing up at school functions and making it a point to chat with the child's teachers. Parents also find that meeting their child's teacher in person makes it easier to voice concerns later, should they arise, and to discuss classroom problems at home with their child.

PARENTS' STRATEGIES FOR SCHOOL SUCCESS

In our interviews with parents, we asked a number of questions about the strategies parents employed when they were concerned about their child's performance in school. One interesting thing we learned from these hundreds of interviews was that parents of successful students used strategies different from those used by parents of unsuccessful students.

If you are a parent, ask yourself this question: what would you do if you learned that your child was doing poorly in some subject at school? Parents of unsuccessful students try to handle the problem themselves, at home. They increase their vigilance over the child's homework, offer to help with assignments, implement more demanding study schedules for the child to follow after school and on weekends, and so on. When this fails, as it typically does, the parents often feel frustrated and get angry at their child. Schoolwork then becomes an area of contention in the household, which only interferes with the child's chances of improving.

Parents of successful students, in contrast, mobilize the school on their child's behalf—they "work the system." When they discover that their child is having a problem with a subject or teacher, they begin by phoning the school and setting up an appointment to meet with the child's teacher, guidance counselor, or principal. They express their concern and offer their assistance in solving the problem. If the school suggests certain home exercises that require the parents' participation, parents of successful students cooperate. But they make it clear that they see their role as helping the school to better serve their child, rather than solving the problem themselves.

There are several reasons for the relative success of "system-work" over "home-work." Perhaps the most important is that parents seldom have the experience or knowledge necessary to solve their child's academic problems on their own. When a child is not performing well in school, the situation could be due to any number of factors; asking the child to study harder may not be the proper solution. Teachers and school counselors, on the other hand, generally have the necessary expertise—and the broader basis of comparison—to diagnose a problem and implement an appropriate solution.

The other reason for the success of "system-work," as opposed to "home-work," inheres, again, in the message that the parents are communicating to the child and school. By working through the school, parents send the child the message that they have faith in the school's ability and willingness to educate the child, and this strengthens the child's belief in the efficacy of school. Moreover, contacting the school when the child is having difficulty lets the school know that the parents are involved and that they expect the school to serve their child. As in dealing with any organization, squeaky wheels get the grease.

THE LOW PREVALENCE OF PARENTAL INVOLVEMENT

Given the importance of parental involvement to student success, it is discouraging to report that very few American parents are as involved in their child's education as they should be. Nearly one-third of the students we studied say their parents have no idea how they are doing in school. About one-sixth of all students believe that their parents don't care whether they earn good grades in school. More than half of all students say they could bring home grades of C or worse without their parents getting upset, and one-quarter say they could bring home grades of D or worse without upsetting their parents. Even if students are wrong in their assessment of their parents' concern, the fact that so many *think* their parents have little interest in their schooling is evidence of a problem of tremendous significance.

In light of the special importance of parents attending school functions, our findings on this type of parental involvement in particular are even more distressing. Only about one-fifth of parents consistently attend school programs. More than 40 percent *never* do. Only one-third of parents regularly attend their child's extracurricular performances, such as athletic events or plays.

Why are so many parents uninvolved in their youngsters' schooling? There are at least three different accounts—one that blames work, one that blames schools, and one that blames parents themselves. All are likely to be true.

First, many parents who wish to be involved are unable to do so, because of demands on their time from work. This is especially a problem in households where each parent is employed full-time, both because work schedules often conflict directly with school schedules (as is the case when school meetings are scheduled during daytime hours) and because working parents must spend their evenings and weekends managing household tasks (shopping, cleaning, laundry, etc.). In our sample, families in which both parents were employed full-time (or, in single-parent homes, in which the single parent was employed full-time) were more likely to be disengaged and less likely to be authoritative than other homes. Not surprisingly, children in these homes were earning lower grades in school as a result.

A second explanation for the widespread disengagement of parents from their children's education has to do with parents' beliefs about their role in their children's education during adolescence. Several national studies of American parents' involvement in their children's education have found a steep drop-off in involvement as children get older. In one national study, for example, the proportion of parents of elementary school students who were involved in their children's education was 50 percent higher than among parents of junior and senior high school students, with the most dramatic decline in parents' involvement occurring around the transition from elementary into secondary school. Interestingly, a similar drop-off in parental involvement does not occur in most Asian countries; if anything, in other countries parents become *more* involved in their children's education as their children get older.

Ironically, the decline in parental school involvement as their children enter adolescence could not occur at a worse time, since, as you will read in the next few chapters, it is just at this point that other forces in youngsters' lives are beginning to compete with school for their time and energy. Nevertheless, far too many parents believe that once their child leaves elementary school, responsibility for managing the child's education is transferred entirely to the school.

Part of the blame for this misapprehension rests squarely on the schools' shoulders. Although schools pay lip service to the benefits of parental involvement, their actual behavior reflects mixed feelings about how much, and in what ways, they actually want parents to be engaged. That is, although schools insist they want parental participation—and complain loudly about the lack of involvement of parents—in actuality, schools only want parents to be involved on the school's own terms. Schools expect parents to monitor and supervise their children's homework and make sure that students show up for school each day and behave themselves while in class—this is what school personnel mean when they say they would like parents to be more "involved." Studies indicate that teachers approve of conferences with parents only when teachers, and not parents, initiate them.

Schools are less willing to share with parents the responsibility for overseeing and managing students' academic careers, and, in fact, they often make it difficult for parents to do so by restricting the amount of information that flows from the school to the home. For example, many schools insist on scheduling parent-teacher conferences for morning and afternoon hours, despite the fact that the vast majority of parents of school-age children are employed full-time. We encountered schools serving newly arrived, Spanish-speaking immigrant families that never offered to conduct programs for parents in Spanish—and yet administrators from these schools wondered why parents never attended back-to-school activities. And we encountered schools that made it impossible for parents to contact the school by telephone to inquire about their child's progress. Some cynical observers believe, perhaps correctly, that schools benefit from parental ignorance, because keeping parents in the dark permits schools to hide whatever mistakes they may make.

Finally, the general lack of involvement by parents in school is reflective of widespread parental disengagement in general. Remember, based on our study and the results of several other national surveys, an estimated one-third of all parents are not really involved in their children's lives. According to our survey, only half of adolescents' parents know their children's friends, what their children do after school, or where their children are when they go out in the evening. Only a third of all parents know how their children spend their spare time or their money. Regardless of whatever complaints we have about schools and the tactics they employ to keep parents less than fully informed, this type of pervasive parental ignorance of their children's day-to-day activities cannot be blamed entirely on educators.

Not long ago, I served as a consultant to a national organization that sponsored a contest in which teenagers were invited to produce their own public service television announcements. The announcements, which were to be in the form of thirty- or sixty-second spots, could deal with any subject that the teenager felt deserved widespread public broadcast, including such topics as drug or sex education, AIDS awareness, conflict management, the importance of staying in school, and so forth. The contest winners would have their announcements broadcast on television.

Hundreds of entries were submitted, from all over the United States. What was the most popular theme? By a wide margin, the most popular message in these spots written and produced by teenagers was one aimed not at their peers, but at parents. The message was devastatingly sad in its simplicity: the adolescents used the public service announcements to remind parents to take time to talk to their teenagers.

PARENTING PRACTICES, SCHOOL ACHIEVEMENT, AND ETHNICITY

As I've noted throughout this chapter, children whose parents use an authoritative style at home—who are warm, firm, and supportive of the adolescent's autonomy—are more engaged and perform better in school. Conversely, students whose parents are disengaged perform considerably worse. I've also noted that the scholastic advantages enjoyed by authoritatively reared students come both from the psychological benefits of growing up in this sort of climate as well as from the greater and more effective involvement of their parents in school.

Given the pattern of ethnic differences in achievement discussed in chapter 5—where, even after taking social class into account, Asian students generally excel relative to other youngsters, Black and Latino students typically lag behind, and White adolescents fall somewhere in between—it makes sense to ask whether these ethnic differences in school performance are due to ethnic differences in parenting. Put concretely, do Asian students succeed in school because their parents do more of the "right" things at home? Do Black and Latino students do poorly in school because their parents do fewer of the right things? Many casual observers of the education scene believe that the answer to both of these questions is an unequivocal yes.

Answering these questions has important implications, not only for our understanding of the roots of ethnic differences in school performance, but also for our understanding of the role of parents in youngsters' education. Programs designed to increase parental involvement in schooling have become enormously popular, and many educators believe that the school performance of low-achieving children could be improved if their parents' behavior were to change. If we were to discover that ethnic differences in parenting were the cause of ethnic differences in achievement, this finding would buttress the argument that more effort ought to be devoted to educating mothers and fathers about effective parenting and to programs aimed at drawing parents into their children's education. Before I reveal our findings, though, I want to say a few words about the meaning of the phrase "effective parenting" and the issue of cultural relativity in defining parental effectiveness.

"EFFECTIVE PARENTING" AND THE PROBLEM OF CULTURAL RELATIVITY

There are some readers who believe that any attempt to define parental effectiveness according to some absolute standard—either in the behavior of the parent or in the development of the child—is arrogant and insensitive to issues of cultural diversity. It is certainly true that different cultural and ethnic groups often hold different values, especially about what is desirable in raising a child. Some cultures are more likely to value obedience, while others are more interested in encouraging self-direction. Some ethnic groups favor a more easygoing, permissive style of parenting, whereas others are stricter and more demanding. And, what is "effective" parenting in accomplishing certain child-rearing goals may be ineffective in accomplishing others. Raising a child to be competitive and strong-willed, for instance, requires a different approach than raising a child to be cooperative and socially compliant.

Given this diversity in parental attitudes and values, is it possible to even talk about what is, and what is not, "effective" parenting? I think it is. That is to say, I think it is possible to specify *some* broad parameters of effective parenting and desirable child outcomes that allow plenty of room to accommodate cultural diversity without being absolutely paralyzed by cultural relativism. Simply put, effective parenting helps prepare the child to live successfully within the society in which he or she will grow up.

Ultimately, then, effective parenting must be judged by taking into account the context in which children are being raised. In our present-day context—contemporary American society—success has become increasingly dependent on doing well in school because educational achievement is so highly determinative of both occupational and economic success. Although there may be cultural groups that do not highly value school achievement, these groups are clearly in the minority in contemporary

America, and their children are at a distinct and real disadvantage. Like it or not, effective parenting must be at least partly defined by the extent to which it encourages and fosters success in school, as measured by school grades, educational attainment, and performance on standardized tests of achievement. We can therefore compare and evaluate different approaches to parenting according to how they affect children's achievement.

ETHNICITY AND ACHIEVEMENT: A PARADOX

Back to our question, then: how are parenting, school performance, and ethnicity related to one another? When we look at the sample as a whole, as I've noted, we find that children from authoritative homes do better in school, and children from disengaged homes do worse, than their peers do. And, when we look separately *within* each ethnic group, we find that the same general pattern holds: In every ethnic group, authoritative parenting is associated with better outcomes, and disengaged parenting with worse ones. White children from authoritative homes perform better in school than White children from authoritarian and permissive homes, who in turn perform better than White children from disengaged homes. Similarly, Latino children from authoritative homes perform better than Latino students from authoritarian and permissive homes, who outperform Latino students from disengaged homes. The same general pattern holds for Asian and Black students, too. In this important regard, then, we have strong evidence that authoritative parenting "works" regardless of the family's ethnic background.

Taken together, these findings are good news for both parents and parent educators, because they suggest that parent education programs designed with one ethnic group in mind are likely to work well for all ethnic groups. We also asked whether authoritative parenting "worked" for poor as well as affluent families, and in divorced as well as nondivorced homes. Again the answer was very encouraging: poor adolescents benefit just as much from authoritative parenting as do wealthy ones, and authoritative parenting works just as well in single-parent homes and in stepfamilies as it does in intact households.

Are differences *between* ethnic groups in children's school performance due to differences in the groups' parenting practices, however? Based on the rank ordering of ethnic groups in terms of student achievement, you would expect that Asian parents would be most involved and most authoritative, and Black and Latino parents least. But, oddly enough, this is not the case.

Consider the comparison between Asian and Black students, for example—two extreme groups in terms of student achievement. According to our surveys, Asian parents are not any more authoritative or any more involved in education than other parents, nor are Black parents any less so. In fact, Black parents, on average, are *more* involved in their children's schooling than are Asian parents—at least in terms of overt participation in school activities—and Black parents are more likely than Asian parents to be authoritative. Yet, despite the ostensibly "better" parenting Black students receive at home, they perform worse in school than Asian students do. Indeed, Asian students from disengaged homes earn grades in school that are higher than Black students from authoritative homes! In other words, although authoritative parenting makes a difference *within* ethnic groups, it does not explain differences *between* groups.*

How is it possible for a factor to make a difference *within* groups but not explain differences *between* groups? Isn't this a contradiction? Not necessarily.

Think, for example, about the relationship between getting a good night's sleep and playing a good game of tennis. If you were to take a group of professional tennis players on the circuit and see if restful sleep the night before a match was related to their performance on the court, you'd almost assuredly find that it was: the players who had slept better would, all other things being equal, probably play better. And, if you were to look at the relation between sleep and tennis performance in a group of tennis amateurs, you'd probably find the same pattern—better sleep at night, better tennis the next day. But even though you had found a relation between sleep and

---

*Although this is mainly true, there is a small exception that pertains specifically to the case of Latino students. When we compare the average parenting observed in Latino households with that observed in other ones, we find that Latino parents are more likely to be disengaged than other parents. This higher level of disengagement is in fact related to the poorer school performance of Latino youngsters.

tennis playing *within* each group (that is, within the group of pros and within the group of amateurs), differences in sleep wouldn't explain differences in the average performance of the professionals and the amateurs. You wouldn't necessarily find that the professionals, on average, had slept better than the amateurs. And, most likely, on any given morning the most well-rested amateur would lose to the most sleep-deprived professional.

In essence, we found that even if you were to expose youngsters from different ethnic groups to the same type of parenting, you'd still find the same pattern of ethnic differences in achievement—just as you'd still find the same pattern of differences in tennis performance if the amateurs and pros got the same amount of sleep. This doesn't mean that parenting (or, for that matter, sleep) doesn't matter—remember that *within each group,* the children with authoritative parents do best, and the children with disengaged parents, worst. It just means that some factor *other than parenting* must account for ethnic differences in achievement and must therefore play a fundamental role in students' success in school.

Even more curiously, we found that the gap between children from authoritative homes and from disengaged homes is not as great within some ethnic groups as it is within others. It is true, of course, that the quality of parenting a child receives matters, for children from all ethnic groups. But it appears as if parenting has more of an impact on student achievement in White homes than it does in Asian, Black, or Latino households.

We looked at this by comparing the grades of students from authoritative versus disengaged homes in each ethnic group. Among White students, the grade difference between students whose parents are authoritative and those whose parents are disengaged is almost a whole letter grade—the difference between earning B's and earning C's. In this group, authoritative parenting has a very strong payoff, at least as far as achievement is concerned. But in Black families, the gap between students from authoritative homes and those from disengaged homes is only about half as large—the difference between earning C's and earning C+'s. And in Asian homes, the gap is even smaller—only one-fourth of a letter grade! It looks as if Asian students' performance in school has very little to do with how their parents raise them.

There is a political cartoon that a student once clipped for me a few years ago—it was published sometime during the Bush administration. The cartoon shows a school-aged student sitting at a dinner table with his mother and father. The student is saying, "Today in school we learned why American students are doing so poorly—it's *your* fault!"

As it turns out, the cartoon is only partly true. Parents are important influences on youngsters' scholastic performance, to be sure, but they are not the whole story. And in some ethnic groups, they are not a very big part of the story at all.

I think this is an enormously important finding, for it challenges a number of widely held, but unproven, assumptions about the reasons for some groups' success in school and for other groups' relative lack of success. Without any hard evidence, we have incorrectly jumped to the conclusion that the remarkable performance of Asian students in school is due to the fact that their parents must be extraordinarily involved in their education. And, by the same token, many observers have looked at the relatively poor showing of Black students and erroneously deduced that the reason is "deficient" parenting. But our findings tell us that these stereotypes are unlikely to be true.

This leads to a sort of "good news, bad news" conclusion. The good news is that, contrary to popular stereotypes, the home environment of Black students, on average, is not typically deficient in ways that are known to harm children's achievement—or at the very least, that the prevalence of "bad" parenting is not substantially higher in Black families than in other groups. On objective measures of parenting, we find that Black parents are just as engaged, and just as involved in their children's education, as other parents are. I think this is good news for all of us interested in education and children's development, but it is especially good news for Black parents, many of whom may have unnecessarily accepted the blame for the higher rate of school problems among their children.

The bad news, though, is that even when Black parents practice the sorts of behaviors that are known to increase children's achievement, their children still do not perform in school at the level of White or Asian students whose parents behave in precisely the same way. Moreover, within Black families, authoritative parenting doesn't have the same positive effect as it does within White families. Something, then, is preventing authoritative parenting from working as well in Black households as it does in White households. This is the subject of chapter 8.

Before we turn to chapter 8, however, I want to draw your attention to an equally curious finding about parenting and school performance that emerged when we looked specifically at the Asian students in our study. It is true, as I noted earlier, that Asian students with authoritative parents perform better than Asian students with average or disengaged parents. But as I've noted, the gap between Asian students from authoritative homes and those from disengaged homes is nowhere as large as it is among White students. In fact, the Asian students from what are ostensibly the worst family environments for school achievement are not performing anywhere near as poorly as we might expect them to be. In the same sense that something in Black households is getting in the way of authoritative parenting working, something in Asian students' lives is preventing "bad" parenting from having deleterious effects.

The factor that undermines the positive effect of effective parenting in Black homes is the same one that counters the adverse effect of ineffective parenting in Asian households—the peer group.

EIGHT

The Power of Peers

Parents play a central role in influencing their child's development and education, but by the time children have reached the later years of elementary school, friends have taken on tremendous importance in their school life. In order to understand the full complement of influences on school performance and engagement, especially during the adolescent years—and in order to understand the causes of America's achievement problem—we need to look closely at the roles played by peers. Indeed, our research indicates that peers shape student achievement patterns in profound ways, and that in many respects friends are more powerful influences than family members are. For a large number of adolescents, peers—not parents—are the chief determinants of how intensely they are invested in school and how much effort they devote to their education.

THE SOCIAL WORLD OF ADOLESCENCE

In our research, we devoted countless hours to investigating and describing the social world of adolescence. This expenditure of time and energy was necessary because studying peer influences on adolescent behavior entails much more than studying the influence of the adolescent's close friends. The close friends a young person has, while significant influences in a young person's life, are only a small part of the total complex of peer influence.

The adolescent's social world can be drawn as three concentric circles. In the innermost circle are the youngster's one or two *best friends*. These are the other children with whom the child spends most of his or her free time—at lunch, during free periods, and so on. If you are the parent of a child between the ages of ten and sixteen, take a moment and think about the children who are your child's best friends. These are the children whom your child greets first on arriving at school, and they are also the children whom your child sees last before leaving school at the end of the day. When the telephone rings for your child on a weekday evening or weekend afternoon, more often than not it is one of these pals.

Best friends comprise the inner circle of the social map of adolescence. In the next circle out are the youngsters who are members of the adolescent's *clique*. These adolescents are also the child's friends, but their friendships are not nearly as intimate as are the ones the child has with his or her closest companions, and these relationships may fluctuate in importance from week to week. At any one time, an adolescent's clique usually will have somewhere between six and ten members. Clique members will sit at the same tables in the school cafeteria, hang around with each other during recess, and interact with each other as they travel to and from class and school. These are the children whose names typically pop up in the stories children share with their parents about the events of the school day.

The third circle in the map of adolescent peer relations is composed of the adolescent's *crowd*. The adolescent's crowd is made up of like-minded individuals who share certain features in common with each other but who are not necessarily each other's friends. Indeed, it is possible for adolescents to be members of the same crowd without really knowing each other well at all. This is because adolescents are members of the same crowd by virtue of their common interests, attitudes, and preferred activities, not because of their relationships with each other. What crowd members have in common is not intimacy, but shared identity. But even though crowd members do not share the intimacy of close friends, they influence each other in important ways. An adolescent may not talk much about the members of his or her crowd, but, as you will read, crowd members greatly influence each other neverthe-less.

THE IMPORTANCE OF PEER CROWDS

When adults tend to think of peer influences on adolescent behavior, they tend to think mainly about influences within the innermost circle (best friends), secondarily about influences in the middle circle (the clique), and only marginally, if at all, about influences in the outermost circle (the crowd). This is quite reasonable, since we might expect that individuals will be most influenced by the people with whom they are closest, and least af-fected by people with whom they share little intimacy. Of course, it is true that during adolescence, as during other periods of life, best friends influ-ence each other's behavior a good deal. But during adolescence, peer influ-ence operates within cliques and crowds in extremely important ways, and adults should probably pay more attention than they do to the ways in which adolescents are influenced by these groups of friends.

It is especially easy to underestimate the power of the adolescent crowd, because its influence is transmitted in less direct, and more subtle, ways than is the influence of the adolescents' close friends or clique. Close friends and clique members influence each other in adolescence much as they influence each other in childhood or adulthood: by providing models whose behavior can be copied ("I'm dressing this way because Jamie looks so cool when she dresses this way"); by rewarding or punishing certain actions, thereby in-creasing (or decreasing) the likelihood of our repeating them ("I'm never wearing this again because Luke laughed at me"); and by exerting direct pressure to behave one way or another ("Jessie told me I just had to wear this shirt to the party"). Crowds, in contrast, are less common in adulthood, and their influence is less familiar to adults.

Because crowd members do not necessarily know each other personally, they don't influence each other directly—through modeling, reinforcement, or coercion. Crowd members influence each other indirectly, through estab-lishing norms and standards that the members feel they must adhere to. Once the adolescent has identified with a particular crowd, the crowd's stan-dards become internalized, incorporated into his or her own sense of self. As a consequence, adhering to the norms and standards of the crowd does not feel to the adolescent like succumbing to peer pressure; it feels more like an expression of his or her own identity.

Adults do not understand this distinction very well. When we think of "peer pressure," we tend to envision an adolescent being coerced by friends to engage in a certain behavior ("Come on, just try this cigarette"), in the company of friends who model a specific action and then wait to be imitated ("Everyone is doing it"), or who actively reward or punish the adolescent for behaving in a given way ("You're not really wearing *that*!"). To be sure, such instances of active peer pressure do indeed occur in the daily lives of teenagers. But much of the peer pressure experienced by adolescents is not this active—nor is it necessarily experienced as pressure—although it is no less powerful in its own way than the more active forms.

PEER PRESSURE PEAKS IN EARLY ADOLESCENCE

The less secure we are about our own identity and our own decision-making abilities, the more we are influenced by others' opinions. But the salience of the crowd as an influence on our behavior declines as we become adults. Because adolescence is a time when individuals often have questions about their identity and their ability to function independently, it is inherently a time of heightened vulnerability to the influence of others. While adults are not immune to pressure from their peers, they are significantly less susceptible to it than adolescents are.

In our research, we have been able to chart changes in individuals' susceptibility to peer pressure as they move into and through adolescence. In several different studies, we have found that vulnerability to peer pressure— that is, how easily swayed a person is by the demands of his or her friends— rises as children become teenagers, peaks sometime around eighth or ninth grade, and then begins to decline as individuals move through high school. There is a specific period in development, then—roughly from age twelve through sixteen—when individuals are easily influenced by their peers. And it is during this time that peers begin to play an enormously important role in influencing achievement.

It is especially interesting to juxtapose the developmental course of peer pressure, with its power peaking in early adolescence, with what we know about the developmental course of parental involvement in schooling. As noted in the last chapter, national studies of American families show that parental involvement drops off precipitously between elementary and secondary school—precisely at the time when youngsters' susceptibility to peer influence is rapidly rising. Moreover, our evidence indicates that this sort of parental disengagement is not limited to school matters, but affects a whole range of issues, including monitoring and regulating the child's relationships with friends, the child's use of leisure time, and the child's choice of activities. To the extent that diminished involvement in their children's lives renders parents' influence less powerful, the door is opened for peers to step in and exert a significant impact on each other's behavior—including their behavior in school. And this is precisely what happens between the sixth and tenth grades. At this point, in fact, children's achievement is more easily influenced by their peers than at any other time in their school career.

SHOULD ADULTS PANIC?

When adults are told that young adolescents are highly susceptible to the influence of friends—and, in fact, that friends may be more potent sources of influence than parents—their first reaction is almost always tinged with anxiety and fear. The stereotype of the adolescent peer group portrays it as an influence that inevitably affects teenagers for the worse—that tempts them into trouble, steers them away from the endeavors that adults value, and coerces them to engage in risky or illicit activities.

In reality, this view of the adolescent's social world is far too simplistic. True, there are peers who encourage their friends to be sexually active or to experiment with drugs, and there are some who cajole their classmates into cutting class or skipping school. But research tells us that there are also teenagers who put pressure on their friends to stay away from drugs, remain committed to school, and refrain from sex, and that these peers can be just as powerful in their influence on other teenagers as peers who are trying to steer other students in the wrong direction. In other words, although peer pressure in early adolescence is a given, *harmful* peer pressure is not.

Friends can influence each other's school performance positively or negatively. As adults suspect, an adolescent whose friends disparage school success will be steered away from scholastic achievement. All other things being equal, a B student whose friends are C students or who are alienated from school, will usually see his or her own grades decline over time as a result of associating with these less academically oriented peers. But, by the same token, an adolescent whose friends value doing well in school will benefit by his or her contact with these peers. That is, a B student whose friends are A students will improve his or her school performance over time as a result of these friendships. Although all adolescents will be influenced by their friends, the specific direction of influence depends on who one's friends are and what they value. Because of this, it is not enough to discuss peer pressure in the abstract—as if it were a monolithic negative influence on adolescents' behavior. We must also know the climate of an adolescent's peer crowd, the characteristics of his or her close friends, and the values held by the members of his or her clique.

Identifying an adolescent's close friends and clique mates is simple enough; we can just ask teenagers to tell us who their best friends are and whom they hang around with. But what about the more amorphous peer crowds? How do we identify the crowds that influence youngsters' behavior?

In order to answer this question in our research, we organized, in each school, a series of small "focus groups" composed of students who represented a cross section of the student body. In these focus groups, we asked students to talk about the main crowds in their school and to identify students who were exemplary members of each of the crowds.

Although we conducted our research in different parts of the country and in very different sorts of schools, we found striking similarities in the types of crowds that were identified in each school. Let's look for a moment at this part of adolescent society.

THE ADOLESCENT SOCIETY

All schools have crowds that emphasize social status, socializing and popularity, although in most schools this group of the socially elite is divided into two somewhat different crowds: "populars" (popularity-conscious students who have a moderately strong commitment to academic achievement but report moderate involvement in delinquent behavior and illicit drug use) and "jocks" (who are quite similar to "populars," but less academically oriented, and not as involved in drug use—except for alcohol, which they often use to excess). Counterbalanced against these elite crowds are one or more alienated crowds—which are referred to by students as "druggies," "burnouts," "greasers," and the like. Along with heavy involvement in drug use and delinquent activities, members of these crowds tend to be inattentive to schoolwork and often hostile toward teachers and other school personnel. Finally, nearly all schools have a large, amorphous crowd, consisting of "average," "normal," or "in-between" students who do not distinguish themselves in any particular area—including school performance.

In addition to these elite, alienated, and average crowds, schools also typically have at least one group of high achievers—so-called "brains" or "intellectuals"—students who thrive on academics, forge close relations with school staff, and avoid drugs and deviant activities. Most schools also feature a very small, socially inept crowd—"loners" or "nerds," as they are often called—whose members are generally low in social status and, consequently, self-esteem.

Although the names of these crowds may vary from school to school, or region to region (e.g., "populars" might be called "preppies," "stuck-ups," or "socies"; "druggies" might be called "freaks" or "stoners"), as far as we can tell, their existence is ubiquitous, at least within public schools. In racially mixed schools, we also find crowds that are defined primarily by ethnicity, and only secondarily by other attributes. For example, some schools have crowds that are characterized by students only as being composed of Black students, or Vietnamese students, or Mexican students, and so on.

Once we had assembled a list of crowds for each of the schools we were studying, we attempted to locate each student in the crowd structure of his or her school. In order to do this, we asked adolescents in each school to classify *other* students, rather than themselves, in the school's crowds. We interviewed several pairs of students in each school and asked them to tell us which crowd each of their classmates was a part of (we prompted them with class lists or yearbook pictures). By repeating this exercise across numerous pairs of raters, we were able to identify most students' crowd affiliation. Although most teenagers say that they themselves are unclassifiable, adolescents have surprisingly little difficulty in identifying which group (or groups) their classmates belong to.

THE PREVAILING NORM: GETTING BY

With this social map in mind, then, what did our study tell us about the peer norms and standards operative within the typical American school? Let's begin by looking at the most common crowds found in American schools and what they stand for. As you will see, there isn't much of a place in the typical American high school for students whose primary concern is academic excellence.

The popularity-conscious, socially elite crowds, whose concerns tend to revolve around socializing, dating, and maintaining social status among friends, account for approximately 20 percent of students in a typical high school. Students in these crowds may do well enough to get by without getting into academic trouble, but they rarely strive for scholastic excellence—most of their grades are B's. Another 20 percent of students belong to one or more of the alienated crowds, where identities are centered around drugs, drinking, delinquency, or defiance; these students are openly hostile to academics—on average, they earn C's. About 30 percent of students describe themselves as "average"—not especially opposed to academic pursuits, but not exactly striving for success, either; like those in the social crowds, their grades hover around straight B's. And between 10 and 15 percent of students belong to a crowd defined by ethnicity, although this figure varies considerably from school to school, depending on the school's ethnic composition. The extent to which members of ethnically defined peer crowds are invested in academics depends largely on the particular ethnic group in question, as I'll explain later in this chapter.

What about the explicitly academically oriented crowds—the "brains," the "intellectuals," and so on? Despite the fact that these students are enrolled in more difficult, more demanding courses—many of them take honors and advanced-placement courses—they maintain an A– average in school grades. But whereas some 70 percent of students belong to one of the solid-B, popularity-conscious elites, one of the low-achieving, alienated crowds, or to the large mass of "average" students, *less than 5 percent of all students are members of a high-achieving crowd that defines itself mainly on the basis of academic excellence.*

Not only is there little room in most schools for the academically oriented, there is substantial peer pressure on students to underachieve. Adults might think that virtually all teenagers would rather do well in school than do poorly, but our studies suggest that this is not necessarily the case. To be sure, the prevailing expectation among American teenagers is that one ought to avoid failing in school and do what it takes to graduate. But our surveys indicate that among American teenagers, there is widespread peer pressure not to do *too* well. For example:

- Although most adolescents say that their friends believe that it is important to graduate from high school (73%) and to go to college (46%), fewer (32%) say that their friends think it is important to get good grades or to go to "one of the best colleges in the U.S." (20%). Nearly as many (16%) say that their friends think it is important that they be "willing to party."
- One out of every six students deliberately hides his or her intelligence and interest in doing well while in class because they are "worried what their friends might think." One in five students say their friends make fun of people who try to do well in school.
- More than one-half of all students say they almost never discuss their schoolwork with their friends. More than one-quarter say they have never studied with their friends. Only one in five has studied with his or her friends more than five times during the past school year.
- We asked the adolescents in our survey to tell us which crowd their friends belonged to and which crowd they'd most like to be a part of. When asked which crowd they would most like to belong to, five times as many students say the "populars" or "jocks" as say the "brains." Three times as many say they would rather be "partyers" or "druggies" than "brains." Of all of the crowds, the "brains" were least happy with who they are—nearly half wished they were in a different crowd.

PEER INFLUENCES ON ACHIEVEMENT

Although the prevailing norm in most high schools is, evidently, to "get by without showing off," there are pockets within each school in which academic achievement is admired, and others in which it is actively discouraged. These cliques and crowds that define a youngster's social world are significant influences on the child's academic performance, because each crowd has its particular set of normative standards and expectations for achievement and behavior in school, and because adolescents attempt to conform to the norms and expectations of their friends. As a consequence, an individual student's school performance will depend in large measure on which crowd the student belongs to, and what that crowd's expectations are for behavior in school. Simply put, given several adolescents of equal scholastic ability, those who are members of intellectual cliques and crowds will achieve more in school than those who are members of the socially elite cliques and crowds, and both groups of adolescents will outperform those who are members of alienated crowds.

This seems reasonable enough, of course—it is hardly surprising that members of academically oriented crowds do best in school and members of alienated crowds do worst. Perhaps it is merely that students who *choose* to associate with brainy classmates are themselves more academically inclined, whereas those that select friends from the alienated crowds are themselves less oriented toward school. After all, it is not as if adolescents are *placed* within different peer groups. How can we be certain that friendships really *affect* students' school performance, rather than simply *reflect* it. Do friends really influence each other—is it really a case of "the company they keep" or is it simply that "birds of a feather flock together"?

By tracking students over a three-year period, we were able to see how they were doing in school at the beginning of the time period, which friends they were spending time with, and whether their school performance and behavior changed over time as a result. By comparing the academic careers of students who began high school with equivalent grades, but who had different sorts of friends during the school years, we were able to see whether the type of friends that adolescents have actually makes a difference in their school performance.

The answer is that it most certainly does, especially in two areas: academic performance and delinquency. Youngsters whose friends were more academically oriented—that is, whose friends had higher grades, spent more time on homework, had higher educational aspirations, and who were more involved in extracurricular activities—did better over the course of high school than students who began school with similar records but who had less academically oriented friends. Similarly, students whose friends were more delinquent—who used more drugs and alcohol and who had more conduct problems—developed more problems themselves over time than did adolescents who began the study with the same behavior profile but who had friends who were less delinquent.

These findings tell us, then, that parents have legitimate reason to be concerned about the qualities and values of their children's friends, especially during early adolescence, when susceptibility to peer influence runs strong. There is also reason to be concerned about the characteristics of the crowd to which an adolescent belongs, since our study found that this influence matters, too. All other things being equal, adolescents who are members of more academically oriented crowds do better in school than other students, whereas those who are members of more alienated crowds do worse and are more likely to get into trouble.

How large a difference do friends make? In one set of analyses, we were able to contrast the influence of best friends with the influence of parents on two important outcomes: the grades in school that the adolescent was getting, and the adolescent's amount of drug and alcohol use. Remember from the previous two chapters that we had found consistent evidence that adolescents from authoritative homes performed better in school and were less involved in problem behavior than their peers. How does the "power of authoritative parenting" stack up in comparison to the "power of the peer group"? *At least by high school, the influence of friends on school performance and drug use is more substantial than the influence of parents' practices at home.* Parents may influence their children's long-term educational plans, but when it comes to day-to-day influences on schooling—whether students attend class, how much time they spend on homework, how hard they try in school, and the grades they bring home—friends are more influential than parents.

The realization that, by high school, peers play as great a role—if not greater—in influencing student achievement and behavior as parents do led us to ask two important questions: First, how do students end up in the crowds to which they belong? Second, does the power of the peer group help explain the consistent ethnic differences in achievement we observed in our study? In other words, is the superior achievement of Asian students, and the inferior achievement of Black and Latino students, due to differences in the peers these youngsters hang out with?

Let's begin by looking at the first question: How do students end up in a specific niche within the adolescent society?

HOW ADOLESCENTS SORT THEMSELVES INTO CROWDS

What is the sorting process through which some adolescents become part of the "brain" crowd and others become "jocks"? What makes some students become "partyers" and others "druggies"? Why do adolescents end up with the particular circle of friends they have?

The results of our study point to three sets of forces that determine in which crowd an adolescent will end up: (1) the adolescent's personality and interests, which in part are determined by the way the student has been raised by his or her parents; (2) the types of peer crowds available to that student in his or her particular school; and (3) the tactics that parents use to "manage" their child's friendships. In describing how these three sets of forces work together, I have found it helpful to use a sort of astronautical metaphor that has three main parts: the launch, the territory, and the navigational plan.

THE LAUNCH

The first set of factors—the child's personality and interests—refers to the general direction in which the child is "launched" as parents prepare to send the youngster on a journey through adolescence. When the child is six or seven, adolescence seems a distant destination, but parents are already "aiming" the child toward certain goals—even if they themselves are not fully aware of what they are doing. As a result of this goal-setting, during the early elementary school years, a sort of "launch trajectory" is established for the child, especially with regard to school matters. Launching the child on a certain trajectory does not guarantee that he or she will reach a particular destination, but it does point the child in a general direction.

At one extreme are children who are launched on a route that is headed in the general direction of educational excellence, instilled with values that stress scholastic success, and who are expected to make school achievement a top priority. In the child's upbringing, traits like perseverance, achievement motivation, and responsibility are emphasized, and parents put into place high standards for achievement. At the other extreme are children whose launch trajectory does not aim the child toward school success. The child may be aimed toward a different goal or, more likely, toward no specific goal at all. Socialization in these households may be overly permissive or inconsistent, and parental expectations and performance standards are unclear. Between these two extremes are other trajectories, which vary in the degree to which they point the child toward school success and in the strength and importance of schooling as an activity.

THE TERRITORY

Because peers play such an important role in influencing children's day-to-day behaviors once they reach adolescence, the territory into which a child is launched—that is, the particular types of peers and peer crowds he or she is likely to run into—is as important as the launch trajectory on which the child is initially placed. Once a child becomes involved with a certain group of friends, these peers begin to have an effect on his or her behavior. To continue the astronautical metaphor, we can think of peer crowds as sorts of "planets" toward which the child is launched. Once a child ends up in the "orbit" of a given peer group, the power of that group keeps the child within its orbit and encourages the child to adopt a certain set of behaviors and outlooks. The longer a child orbits around a certain group of friends, the tighter the rein the group has on the child's behavior, and the more established that behavior pattern becomes.

We saw this quite clearly when we looked at adolescent drug use. The most important determinant of an adolescent's initial experimentation with drugs—primarily alcohol and marijuana—is the home environment. Specifically, adolescents are more likely to begin drinking and experiment with marijuana when they come from households that are exceptionally permissive or in which the parents are disengaged, and they are less likely to experiment with these substances when their parents are authoritative. This is not very surprising. But it is the peer group, and not the home environment, that determines whether an adolescent will progress from experimentation with drugs to regular use. Adolescent "experimenters" who had drug-using friends were far more likely to become regular users than were "experimenters" whose friends were not using alcohol or other drugs. In other words, parental permissiveness or disengagement may launch an adolescent in the direction of drug-using peer groups, but whether drug use becomes a part of the adolescent's regular pattern of behavior depends largely on the peer group that he or she joins. An adolescent from a permissive family who does not connect with a drug-using peer group is unlikely to get into trouble with drugs, despite the permissive home environment.

We can apply the same logic to understanding the dual roles of parents and peers in school achievement. Parents may launch their child on an academic trajectory, but if there is no academically oriented crowd for that student to connect up with, the launching will have little effect. On the other hand, if there are *only* academically oriented peer crowds in a given setting, what parents do at home, in terms of the trajectory they launch their child on, will make relatively less difference, since their child will likely end up in a crowd that emphasizes school success anyway.

To a certain extent, then, the impact of the home environment on the adolescent's behavior will depend to a large measure on the peer groups that inhabit the adolescent's social world. Knowing this helps us understand why the impact of parents on their children's achievement, while significant, is not all-powerful. Parents may socialize a child in a certain direction, but whether that socialization will be successful—that is, whether the adolescent will actually reach the desired goal—will also depend on the peer influences he or she encounters during the journey. This, in turn, will depend on which peers are available for the child to associate with, and how the adolescent navigates among the different circles of classmates within his or her school.

NAVIGATING THROUGH THE ADOLESCENT SOCIETY

Although it is true that parents have less of a *direct* effect on their children during adolescence than during childhood, our studies show that parents can have a powerful *indirect* effect by steering the child toward some peer groups and away from others. Through such piloting, parents can exert some control over the types of peers their child spends time with and, consequently, over the peer influences to which their child is exposed.

There are two chief ways in which parents do this. One way is by attempting to exert some control over the child's choice of friends and out-of-school activities. This, of course, is difficult once the child has entered adolescence, but it is not impossible. Indeed, in contrast to the widely held view that there is little parents can do when it comes to influencing their child's choice of friends, we find in our research that families vary a great deal in the extent to which parents monitor and regulate their child's friendships. More important, parents who exercise greater control over which peers their children spend time with have children who do better in school and who are less likely to get into trouble.

A second, and potentially more powerful, way in which parents influence their child's choice of friends is by selecting the settings in which their child will spend time—by living in one neighborhood as opposed to another, by choosing one school over another, and by involving the child in certain types of after-school and weekend activities. This is really a matter of playing the percentages, trying to maximize the number of "good" peers a child comes into contact with and minimizing the number of "bad" peer influences in the child's environment. When parents maximize the number of good peers in their child's environment, they are less likely to need to exert control over their child's choice of specific friends, since the odds are good that by chance alone the child will come into contact with peers who are likely to be positive influences on his or her development. In essence, although parents can't choose their children's friends, they can influence their child's choices by defining the available pool of possible peers. One way that parents can do this is by making sure that their child's world is adequately populated with other children who themselves have been raised in authoritative families—families that, as I have explained, tend to produce the most well-adjusted children.

WHY NEIGHBORHOODS MATTER

A clear example of this phenomenon was revealed when we looked at how neighborhoods affect children's behavior and performance in school. Because our sample was so large, we were able to compare adolescents who went to the same school but lived in different neighborhoods within the school district. What we found was that adolescents who live in neighborhoods in which a large proportion of families are authoritative perform better in school and are less likely to get into trouble than adolescents who come from identical home environments—and who go to the same school—but who live in neighborhoods in which the population of authoritative families is much lower.

Why would growing up in a particular neighborhood matter, above and beyond the influence of the home and school environment? Because where a family lives affects the pool of peers their child comes into contact with, and this, in turn, influences the child's behavior. If you are a good parent and you live in a neighborhood with other good parents, chances are that the lessons you have tried so hard to teach your child at home will be reinforced when your child comes into contact with other children, and other adults, in the community.

I want to stress here that choosing a "good" neighborhood in which to settle and raise a family is not the same as choosing an affluent neighborhood. Although, as a general rule, the prevalence of authoritative parenting rises, and that of disengaged parenting falls, as one moves up the socioeconomic ladder, parenting style and family income are by no means perfectly correlated. Within any particular social class range, therefore, there is considerable variability in how children are raised, and it is possible both for a well-to-do family to end up in a terrible neighborhood (so far as the quality of parenting is concerned) and for a family of more modest means to end up in a neighborhood that provides a wonderful social environment for children.

What specific factors increase the likelihood that a given neighborhood will provide a good social environment for the child? Based on our research, parents should look for a high level of parental involvement in the local schools, a high level of parental participation in organized activities serving children (sports programs, arts programs, etc.), and a high level of parental monitoring and supervision of children. Our research shows that children who grow up in such neighborhoods fare better. Even if their *own* parents are not especially involved in school, active in their child's life, or vigilant supervisors of their child's activities, the children benefit from contact with peers whose parents have these characteristics. And for parents who *are* involved, active, and vigilant, living in a community in which there is a high proportion of like-minded parents gives an added boost to the beneficial effects of an authoritative home environment.

SCHOOL CHOICE: CHOOSING SCHOOLS OR CHOOSING PEER GROUPS?

Our findings on the importance of peers as influences on adolescent achievement and behavior are interesting in light of current debates about school choice. Most debates about proposals to increase parents' choice of schools—for example, tuition tax credits, giving parents vouchers to use for private school tuition, or permitting parents to choose among several public schools within their area—have focused on the impact of these policies on schools' practices. Proponents of school choice have argued that permitting parents to choose among schools—either among private and public schools, or among only public schools—will enhance school quality because it will force schools to compete with each other. Opponents of school choice programs contend that providing parents with vouchers to use for private schools will undermine the quality of public schools (by siphoning resources out of schools' coffers and directly into parents' hands). In addition, opponents argue that encouraging competition among public schools will ultimately widen the gap between good schools and bad ones, since the good ones, over time, will become more selective and attract better and better students, while the bad ones will ultimately have to serve a larger and larger proportion of ill-prepared students.

An important part of the case made by school choice proponents is the observation that students attending private schools outperform those in public schools. One of the most important elements of this argument is that the observed achievement difference between private and public school students persists even after taking into account the different family backgrounds of these two groups of students (as one would expect, private school students, on average, come from more affluent families). The usual interpretation of the achievement differential between students from private schools and those from public ones is not, then, that the students attending the two kinds of schools are inherently different from each other, but that private schools have higher standards, more rigorous requirements, and more strenuous disciplinary practices. As a consequence, it is argued, students attending private schools take more demanding courses, work harder, behave themselves better, and, ultimately, learn more in school and perform better on achievement tests.

An equally plausible alternative, though, is that the achievement differential between public and private high school students is not due to differences between their families *or* between their schools, but to differences between their peer groups. Comparisons that take family background into account do not control for the more intangible factors that distinguish students who are sent to private school from those who attend public school, such as motivation, self-reliance, and the knowledge that one's parents have made a financial sacrifice for one's education. In all likelihood, students who attend private and parochial schools are exposed to a higher proportion of peers with high educational aspirations and good study habits, and this exposure positively affects their own behavior, entirely independent of the instructional climate of the school. Although our study did not include students from private schools, our findings on the importance of peers, as well as a wealth of research on the minimal effects of school differences on student achievement, are consistent with this interpretation.

When parents are choosing a school, they are not only choosing a principal, a school facility, and a faculty. They are also choosing classmates—and potential friends—for their child. Our study suggests that it may be this aspect of school choice—the choice of a peer group—that may be the most important, and that parents should keep this in mind when selecting a school for their child.

ETHNIC DIFFERENCES IN ACHIEVEMENT: THE IMPORTANCE OF PEERS

Our findings on the importance of peers in adolescent achievement also bear directly on the question of ethnic differences in school performance. Remember, one of the puzzles we encountered when we looked at the role of the family in school achievement was that Asian parents did not, on the surface, appear to be doing anything particularly special that would account for their children's remarkable success, nor were Black parents doing any-thing noteworthy that would explain their children's relatively weaker per-formance. Overall, Asian students in our study were performing better than we would expect on the basis of their parents' practices, and Black students were performing worse. Something in Asian students' lives protects them, even if they are exposed to less than perfect parenting, while something in Black students' lives undermines the positive effects of parental involvement and authoritativeness.

According to our study, this "something" is the peer group. One clear reason for Asian students' success is that Asian students are far more likely than others to have friends who place a great deal of emphasis on academic achievement. Asian-American students are, in general, significantly more likely to say that their friends believe it is important to do well in school, and significantly less likely than other students to say that their friends place a premium on having an active social life. Not surprisingly, Asian students are the most likely to say that they work hard in school to keep up with their friends.

Asian students' descriptions of their friends as hardworking and aca-demically oriented are corroborated by information we gathered indepen-dently from the friends themselves. You may recall that one of the unique features of our study was our ability to match information provided by ado-lescents with information provided directly by their friends. This provided us with a more accurate assessment of each adolescent's social network than would have been possible had we been forced to depend on adolescents' *per-ceptions* of their friends' behavior, since such perceptions can be erroneous (like adults, adolescents tend to overstate the degree of similarity that exists between their friends and themselves).

When we look at friends' activity patterns for adolescents from different ethnic groups, we see quite clearly that the friends with whom Asian stu-dents socialize place a relatively greater emphasis on academics than other students do, whereas the opposite is true for Black and Hispanic teenagers. Specifically, Asian students' friends have higher performance standards (that is, they hold tougher standards for what grades are acceptable), spend more time on homework, are more committed to education, and earn consider-ably higher grades in school. Black and Hispanic students' friends earn lower grades, spend less time on their studies, and have substantially lower performance standards. White students' friends fall somewhere between these two extremes on these various indicators.

When I first saw these findings, my presumption was that they were due entirely to racial segregation in adolescent peer groups. In other words, if Asian students are performing better in school than other students, and Black and Hispanic students worse, and if peer groups are constituted mainly along ethnic lines, it necessarily follows that Asian students will have friends who are doing better in school, and Black and Hispanic students will have friends who are doing more poorly.

It turns out that the segregation argument is only partly true. While it is certainly the case that adolescent peer groups are characterized by a high degree of ethnic segregation—about 80 percent of White and Black students, and more than half of Asian and Hispanic students have best friends from the same ethnic group—there are sufficient numbers of cross-racial friendships in any school to ask whether the pattern described above holds for students who travel in integrated circles. The answer is that it does, at least for the most part. Even if we look solely at youngsters whose best friends are from a different ethnic background, we still find that Asian students' friends place a greater emphasis on doing well in school, and Black and Hispanic students' friends, relatively less. Once again, White students fall somewhere in between.

Peer pressure among Asian students and their friends to do well in school is so strong that any deficiencies in the home environment—for example, parenting that is either too authoritarian or emotionally distant—are rendered almost unimportant. It is, of course, true that Asian students from authoritative homes perform better in school than those from disengaged ones. But an Asian student who comes from a less-than-optimal home environment is likely to be "saved" from academic failure by falling in with friends who value academic excellence and provide the necessary support for achievement.

Why is it so likely that an Asian student will fall into an academically oriented peer crowd and benefit from its influence? Ironically, Asian student success is at least partly a by-product of the fact that adolescents do not have equal access to different peer groups in American high schools. Asian students are "permitted" to join intellectual crowds, like the "brains," but the more socially oriented crowds—the "populars," "jocks," and "partyers"—are far less open to them. For example, whereas 37 percent of the White students in our sample were members of one of these three socially oriented crowds, only 14 percent of the Asian students were—even though more than 20 percent of the Asian students said they *wished* they could be members of these crowds (slightly less than one-third of the White students aspired to membership in one of these crowds). In essence, at least some Asian students who would like to be members of nonacademically oriented crowds are denied membership in them.

A similar argument has been advanced by several Asian social scientists in explaining the extraordinary success of Asian-American students. They have noted that academic success is one of the few routes to social mobility open to Asians in American culture—think for a moment of the relative absence of Asian-American entertainers, athletes, politicians, and so on. For Asian youngsters, who see most nonacademic pathways to success blocked off, they have "no choice" but to apply themselves in school. This is why Asian students are so much more likely than other youngsters to subscribe to the belief that academic failure will bring terrible consequences. When individuals believe that there are few opportunities to success through routes other than education, doing well in school becomes that much more important.

Because Asian students find it more difficult than White students to break into the more socially oriented crowds, they drift toward academically focused peer groups whose members value and encourage scholastic success. The result of this drift is that a large number of Asian students, even those who are less academically talented than their peers, end up in crowds that are highly oriented toward success in the classroom. Once in these crowds, Asian students benefit tremendously from the network of academically oriented peers. Indeed, one of the striking features of Asian student friendships is how frequently they turn to each other for academic assistance and consultation.

The opposite is true for Black and Latino students, who are far more likely than other students to find themselves in peer groups that actually devalue academic accomplishment. Indeed, peer pressure among Black and

Latino students *not* to excel in school is so strong in many communities—
even among middle-class adolescents—that many positive steps that Black
and Latino parents have taken to facilitate their children's school success are
undermined. In essence, much of the good work that Black and Latino parents are doing at home is being undone by countervailing pressures in their
youngsters' peer groups. As a consequence, parental efforts in these ethnic
groups do not have the payoff that we would expect.

This is true not only in racially integrated schools, but in segregated
schools as well. In one well-known study of an all-black, inner-city high
school, for example, the researchers found that students who tried to do well
in school were teased and openly ostracized by their peers for "acting
White." Students were criticized—accused of acting as if they were "better"
than their peers—if they earned good grades, exerted effort in class, or attempted to please their teachers. Those who wished to do well academically
were forced to hide their success and to develop other means of maintaining
their popularity among classmates in order to compensate for being good
students, such as clowning around in class or excelling in some athletic activity. Why would Black and Latino peer groups demean academic success?
In many minority peer groups, scholastic success is equated with "selling
out" one's cultural identity, as some sort of surrender to the control of
White, middle-class America.

I found this so interesting that I asked an extremely bright African-
American undergraduate in one of my seminars at Temple University, who
was familiar with our research, to help me better understand this phenomenon. The student said that the finding rang true for her. She had been raised
in dire poverty within inner-city Washington, D.C., and she was the only
one of her school friends to have made it out of the ghetto; as she explained,
all of her former schoolmates were either on drugs, in jail, on welfare, or
raising an infant. She was torn about where she would settle after graduating from college; the pull to return to her home community was very strong,
but she felt that she could not face her former friends. Whenever she returned home during school vacations, she was taunted for thinking too
highly of herself and teased for not yet having given birth to a child. She said
that the pressure her friends put on her over the years to drop out of college
and return to her roots was enormous. In fact, she said, her friends inti-

mated that the only reason she had gone off to college and avoided early pregnancy was because she was not physically attractive enough to interest a man.

Why is succeeding in school equated in some circles with "acting White" or "selling out"? As Signithia Fordham and John Ogbu, two African-American social scientists who have studied this phenomenon explain:

> [W]hite Americans traditionally refused to acknowledge that black Americans are capable of intellectual achievement, and . . . black Americans subsequently began to doubt their own intellectual ability, began to define academic success as white people's prerogative, and began to discourage their peers, perhaps unconsciously, from emulating white people in academic striving, i.e., from "acting white.

One of my colleagues at the University of Georgia, Layli Phillips, points out that this message—that academic success is somehow incompatible with a healthy Black identity—is perpetuated by a mass media that emphasizes and glorifies low-income African-American peer culture, making it attractive even to middle-class African-American youngsters. African-American parents who want their children to succeed in school are not only battling the force of the Black peer culture (which in many circles demeans academic success), but are fighting a difficult battle against the very powerful images of anti-intellectual Black youth portrayed as normative in music, movies, and television.

We heard variations on the "acting White" theme many, many times over the course of our interviews with high school students. The sad truth is that many students, and many Black students in particular, are forced to choose between doing well in school and having friends. Although there are crowds within each high school in which academic success is valued and in which successful students are respected, these crowds tend to be dominated by White students, and peer groups in American high schools are so ethnically segregated that it is extremely difficult for Black and Latino students to join these crowds. Thus, in many schools, there is a near-complete absence of identifiable peer groups that respect and encourage academic success and are genuinely open to Black and Latino students. As a consequence, it is far more difficult for a talented African-American student than it is for a comparably skilled Asian or White student to find the necessary peer support for achievement.

Among the high-achieving Black students in our sample, for example, only 2 percent said their friends were members of the "brain" crowd, as opposed to 8 percent of the White students and 10 percent of the Asian students with the same grades in school. Interestingly, the proportion of high-achieving Black students who said they *wished* they were members of the "brain" crowd (6 percent) was about the same as it was for White students (5 percent). Thus, while just as many Black students as White students aspire toward membership in the "brain" crowd, membership in this group is more open to White than to Black students.

It is important to understand that the pressure against academic excellence that is pervasive within Black and Latino peer groups is not unique to these ethnic groups. Rather, what we see in these peer groups is an extreme case of what exists within most White peer groups as well. As noted earlier, the prevailing norm in most adolescent peer groups is one of "getting by without showing off"—doing what it takes to avoid getting into trouble in school, but at the same time shunning academic excellence. The chief difference appears to be not in the different ethnic groups' avoidance of excellence—this is common among all but the Asian youngsters—but in how the different ethnic groups define academic "trouble."

We measured students' perception of this "trouble threshold" by asking them what the lowest grade was that they could receive without their parents getting angry. The students' answers to this question confirmed our suspicion: Among Black and Latino students, not until their grades dipped below a C– did these adolescents perceive that they would get into trouble. Among White students, however, the average "trouble threshold" was one entire letter grade higher—somewhere between a B and a C. And among Asian students, the average grade below which students expected their parents to become angry was an astounding A–! One reason for the relatively poorer school performance of Black and Latino students, then, is that these students typically have different definitions of "poor" grades, relative to their White and Asian counterparts. And because peer crowds tend to be ethnically segregated, different normative standards develop within Black and

Latino peer groups than in other crowds. Conversely, one reason for the re-markable success of Asian students is that they have a much stricter, less for-giving definition of academic failure than their Black, White, and Latino peers, and this definition shapes peer norms.

Our findings suggest, then, that a large part of ethnic differences in high school achievement does not derive from differences in the ways in which parents from different ethnic groups raise their children—that is, the "launch" they get from the home environment—but come instead from dif-ferences in the peer environments—the "territory"—that youngsters from different backgrounds encounter. At a time in development when children are especially susceptible to the power of peer influence, the circle of friends an adolescent can choose from may make all the difference between excel-lent and mediocre school performance.

NINE

All Work and All Play Makes
Jack a Dumb Boy

Most of the discussion stimulated by the widely publicized international achievement comparisons—comparisons that favor students from countries other than the United States—has focused on differences between American schools and those in other countries. At one time or another during the past decade, the inferior performance of American students has been attributed by various commentators to deficiencies in our schools' organization, standards, curriculum, schedules, instructional methods, or some other shortcoming in our system of education.

Our schools may, in fact, be inferior to those in other countries in one or more respects, although many of these deficiencies have been greatly overstated. And it may even be the case that one or more of these shortcomings is the root cause of our students' poor showing in international achievement competitions—although attempts to remedy these failings have not resulted at all in better student achievement.

But in attempting to account for the relatively poor showing of American students, we have overlooked one of the most important differences between American high school students and their counterparts in other industrialized countries—a difference that actually has nothing to do with the schools they attend.

American youngsters spend far more time than students in other countries on nonacademic activities—such as part-time work, extracurricular activities, and socializing with friends—and far less time on school-related affairs, such as homework, studying, and reading. The ultimate source of our achievement problem may be how students spend their time *out* of school.

In other industrialized countries, school comes first, and activities such as part-time work or socializing with friends are relegated to any hours left over after school and homework have been completed. In the United States, though, the reverse is the norm: American students manage their academic schedules to fit into their work and play schedules, rather than vice versa. Given the large amounts of time American teenagers devote to their after-school jobs (on average, 15 to 20 hours per week), socializing (another 20 to 25 hours), extracurricular activities (about 15 hours), and watching television (about 15 hours), it is a wonder that they have any time for studying at all. (Fortunately for American adolescents, as we've seen, our schools expect very little of them.)

The amount of time American teenagers devote to more intellectual or academic pursuits is quite meager. On average, American adolescents spend less than 1 hour each week reading for pleasure, and one-fourth of high school students say they never read at all. Seventy percent of high school students devote less than 5 hours weekly to homework, while only 5 percent spend 20 hours or more each week on their studies outside of school.

One reason for our country's achievement problems is that our youngsters spend a disproportionately large amount of their free time in activities that not only fail to support, but that actually detract from, their academic careers. One of the worst offenders is after-school employment.

AMERICAN STUDENTS ARE WORKING TOO MUCH IN PART-TIME JOBS

It is virtually impossible to walk into a fast-food restaurant or shopping mall these days without seeing firsthand how pervasive teenage employment is in America. Indeed, student employment has become so commonplace in this country that it is hard to recall a time when an after-school job wasn't assumed to be a necessary component of an adolescent's life—and it is equally difficult to remember an era when store clerks were generally over eighteen years of age. We need only look back to the 1950s, though, to see that things were not always the way they are today.

For most of the first half of the twentieth century, the worlds of school and work were separate spheres in the lives of American teenagers. As a rule, those who inhabited one realm spent little time in the other. Youngsters who came from families that needed their children's labor in order to make ends meet remained in school for as long as they could, but they typically left before graduating in order to enter the labor force and contribute to their family's income. Those who were more affluent, whose families could make do without their labor, remained in school for virtually all of adolescence; they might have taken on summer jobs or done occasional paid work around the neighborhood, but their lives were structured around school. In essence, some adolescents were students, and others were workers, and there was little overlap between these roles. What changed during the first half of this century were the relative proportions of adolescents who were students *or* workers, as more and more young people found it economically possible to stay in school for longer periods of time. As a result, over time, the proportion of teenagers who were students rose, while the proportion who were workers fell.

Beginning in the mid-1950s, however, and continuing through the early 1980s, a dramatic transformation in the nature of American adolescence occurred that has had far-reaching ramifications on scholastic achievement: it became the norm for students to work in part-time jobs during the school year. How dramatic was the change? Prior to 1950, less than 5 percent of students had school-year jobs. By 1980, though, the world of work had become a salient and significant context for the vast majority of American adolescents, even among those who were enrolled in high school.

The widespread employment of American high school students in part-time jobs is particularly relevant to our discussion of scholastic achievement because, unlike socializing and television viewing, employment is an adolescent activity that adults have a great deal of control over, as parents, educators, and employers. Yet despite the results of many research investigations indicating that intensive part-time employment during the school year takes a toll on student achievement, we continue to permit, if not actively encourage, students to work while attending school. American students' excessive commitment to after-school jobs is an important contributor to the achievement problem we currently face in this country.

It is difficult to obtain precise figures on the prevalence of school-year employment in the United States today. Official government reports from the Department of Labor indicate that around 40 percent of high school students work during the school year, but there is good reason to suspect that this is a substantial underestimate. For one reason, this figure comes from surveys of employers, who have many reasons to underreport the employment of minors. According to media reports, there is widespread violation of child-labor laws by employers of young people (violations concerning the employment of underage workers, the employment of young people in dangerous occupations, and the employment of young people for long hours), and these violations likely lead to the underreporting of adolescent employees, and especially of student employees who are paid "off the books."

Another reason to doubt Labor Department reports comes from surveys of teenagers and parents. School- and home-based surveys indicate that the number of student workers is considerably higher than the employer-derived figures suggest. In fact, most student surveys yield estimates of teenage employment that are about twice the official rates published by the Department of Labor.

Based on our own research, as well as other, well-conducted national and regional surveys of students, we conclude that sometime during their high school career more than 80 percent of American high school students have paying part-time jobs during the school year. During any given school year, approximately 65 percent of high school students work, approximately one-third on any particular day.

AN UPHILL BATTLE

For close to twenty years now, my colleagues and I have been making the argument in scholarly journals and in the popular press that American students work at part-time jobs far too much for their own good, or, for that matter, for the good of the nation. Despite what is compelling evidence supporting this position, it has been incredibly difficult to persuade people that we need to do something to limit student employment if we are going to turn our country's record of poor achievement around. Some progress has been made in a few states, but we still have a long way to go.

One reason for the uphill nature of the battle against excessive student employment is the tremendous power wielded by the industries that are the major employers of teenagers—restaurants, supermarkets, and retail stores. These employers thrive on the inexpensive part-time labor provided by American students. Not surprisingly, they continue lobbying legislators to keep child labor laws loose, waging a concerted public relations campaign designed to convince American parents and students that adolescents somehow reap characterological, if not moral, benefits from spending their afternoons and evenings flipping hamburgers, stuffing burritos, and operating cash registers. What these employers are not so forthcoming about is research showing that the widespread employment of teenagers, while economically beneficial to their industries, is costing the country dearly in depressed student achievement.

Another reason that it has been so difficult to sway those who believe that students ought to have part-time jobs is the antiquated and incorrect image most people have of the student worker. Most adults imagine a poor or lower-class youth struggling to help fill the family coffers or save for further education. They picture youngsters working at a job, perhaps on Saturdays or an occasional weekday afternoon, that will help form a bridge into the adult labor force someday—a sort of modern-day apprenticeship. Part-time employment is seen as serving important economic and educational functions. In reality, however, this picture could not be further from the truth.

First, the typical teenage worker is not a poor youth, but a suburban high school student from a solidly middle-income, if not actually well-to-do, family. Contrary to popular stereotype, working students are not mainly poor youngsters who are working because their families need their earnings, but middle-class youth who are working for additional pocket money to spend on themselves. National surveys show that almost none of the typical student worker's earnings goes toward family expenses or into a college savings account. Most of it goes toward clothing, cars, stereo equipment, and socializing. In our study, for example, close to 60 percent of the workers we surveyed said they spent most or all of their earnings—on average, somewhere between $200 and $300 monthly—on immediate personal expenses. Only about 10 percent said they saved most or all of their earnings for college, and only 3 percent said they gave most or all of their earnings to their family.

Second, in contrast to the picture of the young apprentice who is learning valuable skills that will be helpful when he or she enters the adult workplace, studies show that a small number of different types of jobs—and distinctively "adolescent" jobs at that—employ a large proportion of today's student workers. Opportunities for learning job skills that will have some future payoff are extremely limited. Most younger adolescents work in one of two jobs—baby-sitting or lawn work—and most high school students work either as restaurant workers or retail store clerks. In our study of high school students, nearly 60 percent of the workers were employed in one of these two occupations—as opposed to the 5 percent who were in skilled or semiskilled jobs that offered training in skills that would be useful in adulthood. Since few high school students will pursue careers as child-care workers, gardeners, food counter workers, or cashiers, it isn't clear that the skills most students are learning in their after-school jobs are easily transferable to their likely adult occupations.

Finally, most students' jobs are not limited to Saturdays or an occasional weekday afternoon. Indeed, the time commitment of students to their jobs is quite substantial. In our sample, more than half of the employed students were working at least 16 hours per week, and nearly one-fourth were working 20 hours a week or more. According to national surveys, the average working sophomore works approximately 12 hours per week and the average working senior, close to 20 hours per week. To put this into somewhat different terms, the typical high school senior works the equivalent of a half-time job on top of a school schedule that may account for more than 30 hours per week on its own. And this does not even take into account time commitments to other activities, such as extracurricular programs or household obligations.

The picture of student employment one should keep in mind when discussing its impact on schooling and achievement in America is not the romanticized vision of the hardworking disadvantaged youngster trying to squirrel a little bit of money away for college or to help out with the grocery bills. Most students work to satisfy personal needs in jobs that offer few opportunities for learning and that have little, if any, connection to the type of work they will do as adults. And by the time they are seniors in high school, many students spend more time on the job than they do in the classroom.

PART-TIME EMPLOYMENT UNDERMINES STUDENTS' COMMITMENT TO SCHOOL

There are a variety of barometers by which one can measure the impact of employment on student achievement, and we used several in our research. We compared the grades of students who work a great deal with those who work in limited amounts or not at all. We also contrasted workers with non-workers, and those who work a lot with those who work a little, on different indicators of their commitment to education, such as how much time they spend on homework, how often they cut classes, or how far they want to go in school. And finally, we looked at the impact of employment on various measures of student engagement, such as how hard students try and how steadily they pay attention in class.

All in all, our research shows that heavy commitment to a part-time job during the school year—say, working 20 hours per week or more—significantly interferes with youngsters' school achievement and scholastic commitment. Students who work a lot perform worse in school, are less committed to their education, and are less engaged in class than their classmates who work less or not at all. For example, in our study, students who were working more than 20 hours weekly were earning lower grades, spending less time on homework, cutting class more often, and cheating more frequently, and they reported lower levels of commitment to school and more modest educational aspirations.

It has become clear from our research, as well as a host of other studies, that the key issue is not *whether* a student works, but *how much time* he or she devotes to a job. Working for more than 20 hours per week is likely to be harmful, but working for less than 10 hours per week does not seem to take a consistent toll on school performance. Most probably, the effects of working for between 10 and 20 hours weekly vary from student to student—some can handle it, while others can't. We should keep in mind, however, that half of all employed seniors, about one-third of all juniors, and about one-fifth of all sophomores work above the 20-hour threshold—indicating that large numbers of students are at risk of compromising their school careers by their part-time jobs. These findings suggest that one reason for widespread student disengagement is the fact that so many students are working at part-time jobs.

In our study, we were able to examine whether working long hours lessens youngsters' commitment to school or, alternatively, whether disengagement from school leads students to work. We did this by following students over time, as they increased or decreased their work hours, and studying how different patterns of employment affected school performance and engagement. When students increase their work hours, does their commitment to school decline as a result? When students cut back on their employment, does their school performance improve?

The answer to both of these questions is yes. While it is true that the more disengaged students are more likely to work long hours to begin with, it appears that working makes a bad situation worse. In other words, over time, the more students work, the less committed to school they become, even if they begin work with a more negative attitude toward school. (Working long hours also adversely affects students who enter the workplace with positive attitudes toward school.) When students withdraw from the labor force, however, or cut back on their work hours, their interest in school rises. The good news, then, is that the negative effects of working on schooling are reversible.

There are several explanations for the negative effects of working on students' engagement in school. First, when students work many hours each week, they have less time to devote to school assignments. According to our studies, one common response to this time pressure is for working students to cut corners by taking easier classes, copying assignments from other students, cutting class, or refusing to do work that is assigned by their teachers. Over time, as these become established practices, students' commitment to school is eroded bit by bit. About one-third of the students in our study said they take easier classes because of their jobs.

Second, in order to work 20 or more hours each week, many students must work on weekday evenings. Evening work may interfere not only with doing homework, but with both sleep and diet—studies show that working teenagers get less rest and eat less healthy meals than nonworking teenagers—and burning the midnight oil may make working teenagers more tired in school. Teachers frequently complain about working students falling asleep in class. Nearly a third of the students in our study said they were frequently too tired from work to do their homework.

Third, it appears that the excitement of earning large amounts of spending money may itself make school seem less rewarding and interesting. Although mind-wandering during school is considered a hallmark of adolescence, working students report significantly more of it than nonworkers. Indeed, the "rush" from earning and spending money may be so strong that students who have a history of prolonged intensive employment—those who, for example, have been working long hours since their sophomore year—are actually at greater risk than their classmates of dropping out before graduating.

Finally, working long hours is associated with increased alcohol and drug use. Students who work long hours use drugs and alcohol about 33 percent more often than students who do not work. Alcohol and drug use, in turn, are linked to disengagement from school, so any activity that leads adolescents to drink or experiment with drugs is likely to depress their school performance. Interestingly enough, our longitudinal studies show that working long hours *leads to* increased alcohol and marijuana use. Teenagers with between $200 and $300 of discretionary income per month have a lot more money to spend on drugs and alcohol than their peers, and this is one of the things they spend their earnings on.

Given the widespread belief that employment during adolescence is supposed to be character-building, it no doubt will come as a surprise to many readers to hear that working at a part-time job *diminishes* students' engagement in school and increases their drug and alcohol use. But studies of how student workers actually spend their time on the job suggest that the real surprise is that we've held on to the myth of the benefits of adolescent work experience for as long as we have.

ONLY IN AMERICA

The United States is the only country in the world in which working during high school is commonplace, especially among students who have their sights set on continuing their education beyond high school. (Some countries, for example, Germany, have formal apprenticeship programs in which students are placed with employers who provide them with genuine career training, but this is quite different from the work experience of the typical American teenager.) Although good comparative data are difficult to come by—student employment is such a rarity in other countries that it is seldom monitored with any regularity—part-time employment during the school year is only about half as common in Canada as in the United States, only about one-third as common in Western Europe, and virtually unheard of in Asia, except among students enrolled in vocational schools. Most telling, ours is the only country in the world that actively encourages large numbers of *college-bound* high school students in particular to take on jobs during the academic year. Other countries encourage their high-achieving students to devote their free time to studying and preparing for college.

Why is student employment so much more prevalent in the United States than in other countries? There are three main reasons. First, employment opportunities for students are far greater here because of our extensive network of retail and service jobs. Retail and service jobs are not as plentiful in other countries, and to the extent that such jobs are available, there is substantial political pressure to target them toward individuals who really need them: adults with families to support or youth who are not enrolled in school. In the United States, most of these jobs are low-wage and part-time, which means that they are ill suited for adults who are trying to support a family or who need the benefits typically associated with full-time employment, such as health insurance. Furthermore, many retail and service employers want workers who can work during off-hours (i.e., on weekends and during evenings) and who can vary their work schedules and work hours from week to week, which also makes these jobs unattractive to adults. In contrast, most teenagers enjoy the scheduling flexibility, are able to work at the times their employers need them to, and are not interested in full-time employment.

Second, American students have considerably more leisure time at their disposal than do students from other countries, who have longer school days (in other countries, school days are one to two hours longer than in America), who must study harder because of their schools' more rigorous curricula, who have less free time available during the school day in which to do homework assignments, and who have far more homework assigned—homework that their teachers actually expect them to complete. Most European and Asian high school students would find it utterly astonishing that their American counterparts have four or five hours of free time each day to devote to an after-school job. And most would find it incredible that the average American teenager spends only about one hour per day on homework.

Finally, and perhaps most important, Americans have an ambivalent view of how young people should spend their time in preparation for adulthood. Because taking on an after-school job is seen by many adults as a sign of diligence—a marker of maturity—it is not easy to criticize adolescents for working, nor is it easy to gain an audience for the argument that American students are probably working more than they should. We are especially enamored in the United States with the idea that "hands-on" learning is superior to "book learning," and that laboring in a "common" job is the best way to build character. Many Americans remain skeptical about the genuine value of what their children are taught in school and are convinced that youngsters learn more in the "real world" than in conventional classrooms.

INVOLVEMENT IN EXTRACURRICULAR ACTIVITIES: HOW MUCH IS TOO MUCH?

Approximately the same number of students participate in school-sponsored extracurricular activities as work during any given school year—each year, roughly two-thirds of all students participate in at least one extracurricular activity. Not surprisingly, athletics account for the largest proportion of extracurricular participants (about half of all adolescents are student-athletes, either at the interscholastic or intramural level); followed by musical organizations, such as band, chorus, or orchestra (about one-quarter of adolescents belong to one of these); and academic or career clubs (about one-fifth of all adolescents belong to one of these).

Of course, many youngsters are involved in organized activities—athletics and otherwise—that are not administered under the aegis of the school. In our survey, we also collected data about participation in various extracurricular activities that were not school-sponsored. Using this more liberal assessment of extracurricular involvement indicates that participation in nonacademic activities during after-school hours is quite pervasive. According to our data, nearly three-fourths of high school students are involved in one or more sports activity (i.e., an additional 25 percent over and above the half who participate in organized school sports), and about 40 percent report participating in organized music or dance activities (i.e., an additional 15 percent over and above the proportion in school-sponsored musical activities).

Although participation in sports and other extracurricular activities is extensive, it is not nearly as *intensive* as students' involvement in part-time work, however. Relatively few students—less than 5 percent, in fact—report spending 20 hours per week or more on school-sponsored extracurricular activities, and this level of commitment tends to be limited to the handful of students involved in either football or basketball. More common are the majority of student-athletes, who report spending between 10 and 15 hours weekly on their sport; participants in music and theater activities (who average between 5 and 10 hours weekly); and members of school clubs (who generally spend only a few hours each week in them). Even if we add the time that students spend in extracurriculars that are not sponsored by the school, the time commitment American teenagers make to organized leisure activities does not really begin to approach the commitment they make to employment. It is substantial, nevertheless.

EXTRACURRICULAR INVOLVEMENT
AND SCHOOL ACHIEVEMENT

One can view teenagers' participation in extracurricular activities in two very different ways. On the one hand, time spent in after-school activities that are explicitly endorsed by the school should, presumably, have a different effect on school engagement than after-school employment. After all, school-sponsored extracurricular activities are often designed to strengthen youngsters' ties (and presumably, their commitment) to their schools, either by helping students develop an emotional attachment to the institution or by creating close personal ties between students and the teachers who serve as coaches or club advisors. This bonding may actually spill over into the academic domain—or so many educators think.

On the other hand, as is the case with after-school employment, commitment to an extracurricular activity takes time—time that might otherwise be directly invested in academic activities. Athletes, for example, especially those in the most visible sports, devote considerable time each week during the playing season to practices, games, and training. The time demands and performance pressures associated with some extracurricular endeavors may leave participants too preoccupied or too fatigued to concentrate on schoolwork. And excellence in an extracurricular activity, while desirable in its own right, may have the unintended effect of obviating the need to work hard on academic material. This is especially likely in schools that lavish attention on exceptional athletes and others who excel in settings outside the classroom.

What do we know about the impact of extracurricular participation on achievement? Recent research shows that any apparent advantages that appear to be associated with extracurricular participation are likely to precede, rather than follow from, involvement in the actitity. In other words, playing sports does not make adolescents better students; on average, students with better academic records are more likely to be involved in extracurricular activities.

But what about the other side of the coin? Is the extensive involvement of American students in organized extracurriculars *hurting* their academic achievement?

Our own research indicates that this is a difficult question to answer. As is the case with part-time employment, students' grades go down when their time commitment to extracurriculars exceeds 20 hours weekly—although, as I've noted, unlike after-school employment, few students clock this much time on extracurriculars. Below this 20-hour threshold, however, it looks like student achievement *increases* modestly with increasing hours of participation. In other words, extracurricular participation—at the level at which most students in this country are engaged—seems to help, rather than hurt, academic achievement.

This statement has to be qualified, though. Much depends on the specific activity pursued. The impact on achievement of participating in "major" sports (such as football and basketball) is rarely positive, and can sometimes be negative, whereas the impact of participating in service, academic, and leadership activities (e.g., student government, newspaper, language clubs) is clearly beneficial. The impact of participation in "minor" sports (wrestling, gymnastics, tennis) and of participation in the performing arts falls somewhere between the two extremes.

Finally, students' performance suffers more when the activity in which they participate directly interferes with school-related responsibilities and it is enhanced when the activity fosters the development of more efficient time-management skills. This helps to explain why participation in major team sports may hurt school performance somewhat. Participation in major sports often leaves students too drained of time and energy to devote sufficient concentration to their studies. Indeed, in many high schools, student athletes are expected to practice both before *and* after school each weekday in addition to the time they devote each week to actual competition. Many athletes report being nervous and distracted during class on days of important games. In our survey, about one-third of the extracurricular participants reported that their participation often left them feeling too tired to do homework and too excited to concentrate in school. On the plus side, about half of all participants reported that their extracurricular participation had made them feel more confident and more organized in their studies. On balance, then, it appears that extracurricular participation has no large impact on academic achievement, in either direction, as long as students don't overdo their involvement to the point that their commitment takes more than 20 hours weekly.

There is an important exception to this general conclusion, however. Although extracurricular participation generally has only a negligible impact on the achievement of average or above-average students, it may actually enhance the achievement of below-average students. Consequently, policies that restrict the extracurricular participation of low-achieving students may hurt, rather than help, their academic performance. In all likelihood, participation in school-sponsored extracurriculars helps bond students to school—particularly those who might otherwise disengage from the institution—and that some of this "bonding" spills over into improved classroom performance.

Ultimately, what probably matters most of all are the values and attitudes students encounter among their teammates and fellow participants. (Interestingly, we do not find that the attitudes of coaches or advisors matter much.) Students who devote a great deal of time to an extracurricular activity spend much of their free time in the company of peers who share that interest. In this regard, we can look at extracurricular participation as yet another factor that affects the peer influence to which students are exposed—and, as we saw in the last chapter, peers exert a tremendous impact on student achievement. When fellow participants value academic accomplishment—as is more often the case in service and leadership activities than in the glory sports—this value is transmitted and reinforced through the informal contact that participants have with each other.

THE HIGH COSTS OF MAINTAINING AN ACTIVE SOCIAL LIFE

In addition to their tremendous investment of time and energy in part-time jobs and school-sponsored extracurriculars, American students, compared to their counterparts abroad, also spend a substantial amount of time socializing with their friends. This time-use difference cannot be attributed simply to the shorter school days of American students (who therefore have more free time outside of school than do students in other countries). The cross-cultural difference in time spent socializing is substantially greater than the cross-cultural difference in time taken up by formal school classes. American students' preference for spending their free time socializing with friends reflects differences in priorities rather than in opportunities.

Excessive television viewing is often blamed for the poor achievement of American youngsters, but as far as we can tell from systematic research, this account is probably not correct. Many readers may be surprised to learn that it is time spent "playing," not viewing television, that most clearly distinguishes American children and adolescents from their counterparts abroad. (By "playing," I mean playing games or sports during childhood, and socializing with friends during adolescence.) While it is true that American youngsters spend a considerable amount of time watching television (somewhere close to 15 hours weekly), this figure is comparable to that reported by youngsters in other countries. This international comparability is not the case when it comes to "playing," however; elementary school children in America spend twice as much of their free time playing as Asian children, for example, and American adolescents spend about twice as much time dating and socializing as do their Asian counterparts.

How much time do American teenagers devote to their social lives? Actual estimates vary from study to study—partly because definitions of "socializing" vary from study to study—but there is no doubt that socializing is the most time-consuming activity on the American adolescent's agenda. Our best estimate is that the average teenager spends between 20 and 25 hours per week socializing with friends, and this does not include the large amount of time at school that is spent in social activities.

American teenagers not only spend more time socializing and dating than do teenagers from other countries. Researchers find differences among countries in what students do while they are with their friends. In the United States, with the exception of the small proportion of students who are members of academically oriented crowds, the worlds of academics and socializing with friends are separate. As noted in the previous chapter, more than one-half of American adolescents say they have *never even discussed* schoolwork with their friends. In the United States, socializing with friends nearly always means recreation, in the form of hanging out, partying, or playing. This is not the case in other countries: for example, one out of five Asian students combines socializing with studying, in contrast to the only 1 percent of American students who put the two activities together. Thus, it is not merely the fact that American teenagers spend so much time socializing that is problematic; the problem is that when American adolescents are with their friends, school-related concerns become virtually nonexistent for all but a small minority of youngsters.

The separation of the worlds of school and peers characteristic of the United States translates into different costs and benefits of socializing here compared with other countries. Because American adolescents virtually never study with their friends and rarely even discuss their schoolwork, time spent socializing among American teenagers is strongly associated with lower grades in school. In one recent study, for example, the amount of time

American teenagers spent socializing with friends was a stronger predictor of poor grades than was the amount of time teenagers spent watching television. This is not the case in Asian countries, however, because socializing often means getting together with friends to study.

Cross-cultural differences in how students spend their time out of school do not emerge for the first time in adolescence, of course. School and school-related activities occupy proportionately more time in the daily lives of children in other countries from an early age. Part of this is due to the greater demands placed on children in other countries for homework, studying, and the like—but part seems to be attributable to international differences in parents' values and priorities. American parents are not enthusiastic about their children being assigned great amounts of homework (indeed, many schools report that parents call and complain when their children are assigned "too much" homework), spend relatively less money on purchases designed to facilitate youngsters' achievement (such as desks), and are more willing to burden their children with household chores than to insist on their devoting time to more intellectual actitivies such as reading.

In one recent study, a sample of mothers from the United States, Hungary, Taiwan, and Japan were asked what they most worried about in relation to their child. The top category of worries mentioned by mothers everywhere but the United States was school-related (e.g., how their child was performing in school, whether their child would get into college). American mothers mentioned school-related worries less often than worries about the child's economic future (e.g., whether their child would make enough money, whether their child would be a success) or about their child's personality (e.g., whether their child had high self-esteem, whether their child was happy).

THE 15 PERCENT SOLUTION

When we assemble various pieces of the time-use puzzle into a larger picture, it is not difficult to see why our students lag behind those from other countries on standardized tests of achievement.

The typical adolescent has about 120 waking hours each week (assuming an average of 7 hours of sleep per night). The average school day in the United States lasts 6.5 hours, accounting for between 30 and 35 hours each week. According to time-use studies, teenagers devote an additional 25 hours each week to eating, personal care, household chores, transportation, and the like.

This leaves somewhere around 60 hours each week for students to apportion across a variety of other activities. If the American typical teenager is devoting between 20 and 25 hours weekly to socializing, between 15 and 20 hours weekly to a part-time job, between 10 and 15 hours weekly to an extracurricular activity, and between 10 and 15 hours weekly to television viewing, there isn't any time left over for studying outside of school—which explains why the national average for time spent on homework is less than 5 hours per week.

When we consider that only 40 percent of the time spent in school is spent on academic activities, it becomes clear that little of the typical American student's time—something on the order of between 15 and 20 hours weekly, or only about 15 percent of his or her waking hours—is spent on endeavors likely to contribute to learning or achievement.

ETHNIC DIFFERENCES IN AMERICAN ADOLESCENTS' ACTIVITY PATTERNS

If it is indeed the case that the work and play schedules of American adolescents are interfering with their achievement in school, we should expect to find that differences *among* students in the United States in their patterns of employment and leisure are related to differences in their levels of academic accomplishment. And this is precisely the case: students who work long hours, devote more than 20 hours weekly to extracurricular activities, and spend a large amount of time socializing with friends earn lower grades and are less committed to school than their counterparts.

We also find ethnic differences in how adolescents spend time outside of school. Compared with their White, African-American, and Latino peers, Asian-American students are less likely to have after-school jobs, less likely to work long hours if they are employed, less likely to devote long hours to extracurricular activities, and more likely to devote time out of school to academic pursuits.

The most noteworthy ethnic difference in patterns of activity is in socializing, however. We asked adolescents to estimate the amount of time they spent in a variety of activities, including "hanging out" with friends, "partying," and "spending time with a boyfriend or girlfriend." According to our data, Asian-American students spend about half as much time socializing as other students do. This is important, because socializing with friends is correlated with lower school grades.

It is not coincidental, then, that Asian students, who earn the highest grades in school, rank lowest on three time-use factors associated with poorer school performance—working long hours at a part-time job, devoting more than 20 hours per week to an extracurricular activity, and spending a great deal of time socializing with friends. Nor is it coincidental that Asian students rank highest on two important time-use factors predictive of school success: spending time on homework and affiliating with friends who talk about schoolwork, study together, and assist each other with school assignments.

At one level, these differences are hardly surprising. Because Asian-American students worry more than other students about the possible repercussions of not doing well in school, they devote more time and energy to their studies and exert more effort on academic activities. This orientation draws them into peer crowds that emphasize school achievement and support scholastic success, where they have regular and frequent contact with other students who share their high level of engagement in school and who strengthen this orientation through collective studying, cooperation on school assignments, and out-of-school discussions about in-school activities.

At another level, though, the findings shed further light on the larger issue of achievement in America and debates about the need for school reform. Student achievement is as much a product of the ways in which children and adolescents arrange and structure their lives—the activities they pursue, the priorities they hold, the endeavors they value—as it is a product of the schools they attend. It is unlikely that school reform, in and of itself, will make school more important in the minds of students. And unless and until students and their parents view success in school as a necessary and worthwhile goal—actually, until success in school *is* a necessary and worthwhile goal in American society—students will not seek it with passion or commitment.

To be sure, schools have some responsibility for shaping students' priorities and influencing their beliefs. By not demanding much of students' time out of the classroom, schools undermine their own cause, because these practices allow youngsters to spend too much time on activities whose goals ultimately clash with the schools' overall mission. A vicious cycle is set in motion: the less schools demand, the more students spend their time earning pocket money and socializing with their friends; the more they engage in these activities, the more their interest in school wanes. Confronted with an increasingly disengaged student populace, schools, like the classic permissive parent, respond by demanding less, lowering standards, and searching for gimmicks to keep youngsters engaged. Unfortunately, this strategy only exacerbates the larger problem.

Yes, schools have played a role in the declining achievement of American students. But the other institutions that touch students' lives—most importantly, the family, employers, and the mass media—have contributed to the problem. For too many American parents, school is simply something their children do, an activity on (and not necessarily at the top of) a long list that includes recreation, athletics, socializing, and part-time employment. To European and Asian parents, school is the defining activity of both childhood and adolescence. Everything else comes second.

TEN

Beyond the Classroom

For nearly fifteen years now, educators and policy-makers have been engaged in a nationwide effort to solve the problem of low student achievement in America. In one blue-ribbon bipartisan commission report after
another, the American public has been told that if we change how we organize our schools, how and what we teach in our classrooms, and how we select, train, and compensate our teachers, we will see improvements in our
children's educational performance. In response to these reports, government agencies and private foundations have spent massive amounts of
money on research designed to transform America's schools. Although we
hear occasional success stories about a school here or a program there that
has turned students' performance around, the competence of American students has not improved.

It is time we faced the music: fifteen years of school reform has not really accomplished anything. Today's students know less, and can do less,
than their counterparts could twenty-five years ago. Our high school graduates are among the least intellectually competent in the industrialized world.
Contrary to widespread claims that the low achievement of American students is not real—that it is merely a "statistical artifact"—systematic scien-

183

tific evidence indicates quite compellingly that the problem of poor student achievement is genuine, substantial, and pervasive across ethnic, socioeconomic, and age groups.

The achievement problem we face in this country is due not to a drop in the intelligence or basic intellectual capability of our children, but to a widespread decline in children's interest in education and in their motivation to achieve in the classroom; it is a problem of attitude and effort, not ability. Two decades ago, a teacher in an average high school in this country could expect to have three or four "difficult" students in a class of thirty. Today, teachers in these same schools are expected to teach to classrooms in which nearly half of the students are uninterested. And only a very small proportion of the remaining half strives for excellence.

Given the findings of our study, it is not difficult to understand why so many students coast through school without devoting very much energy to schoolwork. As things stand, there is little reason for the majority of students to exert themselves any more than is necessary to avoid failing, being held back, or not graduating. Within an educational system in which all that counts is promotion to the next level—in which earning good grades is seen as equivalent to earning mediocre ones, and worse yet, in which actually learning something from school is seen as equivalent to not learning anything at all—students choose the path of least resistance. Getting by, rather than striving to succeed, has become the organizing principle behind student behavior in our schools. It is easy to point the finger at schools for creating this situation, but parents, employers, and the mass media have been significant participants in this process as well.

Our findings suggest that the sorry state of American student achievement is due more to the conditions of students' lives outside of school than it is to what takes place within school walls. In my view, the failure of the school reform movement to reverse the decline in achievement is due to its emphasis on reforming schools and classrooms, and its general disregard of the contributing forces that, while outside the boundaries of the school, are probably more influential. In this final chapter, I want to go beyond the findings of our study and discuss a series of steps America needs to take if we are to successfully address the problem of declining student achievement.

LESSONS FROM THE STUDY OF ETHNIC DIFFERENCES

Although we did not intend our study to be a study of ethnicity and achievement, the striking and consistent ethnic differences in performance and behavior that we observed demand careful consideration, if only because they demonstrate that some students are able to achieve at high levels within American schools, whatever our schools' shortcomings may be. This does not mean, of course, that our schools are free of problems, or that all students would be performing at high levels "if only" they behaved like their successful counterparts from other ethnic groups. Nevertheless, our findings do suggest that there may be something important to be learned by examining the behaviors and attitudes of students who are able to succeed within American schools as they currently exist, and that something other than deficiencies in our schools is contributing to America's achievement problem.

By identifying some of the factors that appear to contribute to the remarkable success of Asian students (and immigrant Asian students in particular), or that impede success among African-American and Latino students (and especially among Latinos whose families have been living in the United States for some time), we were able to ask whether these same factors contribute to student achievement in all groups. That is, we asked whether the factors that seem to give an advantage to Asian students as a group are the same factors that facilitate student achievement in general, regardless of a youngster's ethnic background. The answer, for the most part, is yes.

Across all ethnic groups, working hard in school is a strong predictor of academic accomplishment. One clear reason for the relative levels of performance of the various ethnic groups is that Asian students devote relatively more effort to their studies, and Black and Latino youngsters relatively less. Compared with their peers, Asian youngsters spend twice as much time each week on homework and are significantly more engaged in the classroom. Students from other ethnic groups are more likely to cut class, less likely to pay attention, and less likely to value doing well in school. Black and Latino students are less likely to do the homework they are assigned than are White or Asian students.

Second, successful students are more likely than their peers to worry about the potential negative consequences of not getting a good education. Students need to believe that their performance in school genuinely matters in order to do well in the classroom, but students appear to be more strongly motivated by the desire to avoid failure than by actually striving for success. Because schools expect so little from students, however, it is easy for most of them to avoid failing without exerting much effort or expending much energy. Within a system that fails very few students, then, only those students who have high standards of their own—who have more stringent criteria for success and failure—will strive to do better than merely to pass their courses and graduate.

Asian students are far more likely to be worried about the possibility of not doing well in school and the implications of this for their future; this, then, is a second reason for their superior performance relative to other youngsters. Contrary to popular stereotype, African-American and Latino students are not especially pessimistic or cynical about the value of schooling, but, rather, are unwisely optimistic about the repercussions of doing poorly in school. Either these students believe that they can succeed without getting a good education or they have adopted this view as a way of compensating psychologically for their relatively weaker performance. In either case, though, their cavalier appraisal of the consequences of doing poorly in school is a serious liability.

Third, there are important differences in how students view the causes of their successes and failures, and these differences in students' beliefs have important implications for how they actually perform in school. Successful students believe that their accomplishments are the result of hard work, and their failures the consequence of insufficient effort. Unsuccessful students, in contrast, attribute success and failure to factors outside their own control, such as luck, innate ability, and the biases of teachers. The greater prevalence of the healthful attributional style we see among Asian students in this country is consistent with what other researchers have found in cross-cultural comparisons of individuals' beliefs about the origins of success. Americans, in general, place too much emphasis on the importance of native ability, and too little emphasis on the necessity of hard work. This set of views is hurting our children's achievement in school.

Regardless of ethnic background, success in school is highly correlated with being strongly engaged in school emotionally. The factors that contribute to the relative success of Asian students—hard work, high personal standards, anxiety about doing poorly, and the belief that success and failure are closely linked to the amount of effort one exerts—are keys to academic success in all groups of students. The superior performance of Asian students in American schools, then, is not mysterious, but explainable on the basis of their attitudes, values, and behavior.

TALES OUTSIDE OF SCHOOL

Our study points to a number of pervasive problems outside of school that must be addressed if any efforts at school reform are to succeed.

The first, and most significant, problem, is the high prevalence of disengaged parents in contemporary America. By our estimate, nearly one in three parents in America is seriously disengaged from his or her adolescent's life, and, especially, from the adolescent's education. Only about one-fifth of parents consistently attend school programs. Nearly one-third of students say their parents have no idea how they are doing in school. About one-sixth of all students report that their parents don't care whether they earn good grades in school or not. Not surprisingly, parental lack of interest is strongly associated with children's academic difficulties and low school achievement. In addition, parental disengagement is a very good predictor of many of the problem behaviors whose levels have reached alarming proportions in the past twenty-five years: alcohol and drug abuse, delinquency and violence, suicide, and sexual precocity.

A second contributor to the problem is a contemporary American peer culture that demeans academic success and scorns students who try to do well in school. The adolescent society in America has never been a strong admirer of academic accomplishment, but widespread parental disengagement has left a large proportion of adolescents far more susceptible to the influence of their friends than in past generations. Although this influence is not always for the worse, more often than not it is. Fewer than one in five students say their friends think it is important to get good grades in school. Less than one-fourth of all students regularly discuss their schoolwork with their friends. Nearly one-fifth of all students say they do not try as hard as they can in school because they are worried about what their friends might think. Today, part of being an American adolescent is adopting a cavalier or derisive attitude toward school. Sadly, the longer a student's family has lived in this country, the less committed to doing well in school he or she is likely to be.

These problems—parental disengagement and a peer culture that is scornful of academic excellence—are compounded by a third: an activity schedule that demands little academic energy from students when they are not actually in the classroom and permits students to devote excessive amounts of time to socializing, part-time employment, and a variety of leisure activities. Very little of the typical American student's time—something on the order of between 15 and 20 hours weekly, or only about 15 percent of his or her waking hours—is spent on endeavors likely to contribute to learning or achievement. In terms of how much time is expected of them for school and school-related pursuits, American students are among those in the industrialized world that have the fewest demands put on them.

Solving America's achievement problem will require a national effort that involves not only schools, but parents, employers, the mass media, and ultimately, students themselves. Based on our study, here are ten recommendations for places to begin a reasonable discussion of the issues:

1. REFOCUS THE DISCUSSION

First and foremost, we must transform the national debate over the causes and cures of our achievement problem from one about reforming schools to one about changing students' and parents' attitudes and behaviors. It is essential that the public understand that no amount of school reform will work unless we recognize the problem as considerably more far-reaching and complicated than simply changing curricular standards or teaching methods.

2. ESTABLISH ACADEMIC EXCELLENCE AS A NATIONAL PRIORITY

We must make it clear in the minds of young people and parents that the primary activity of childhood and adolescence is schooling. If we want our children and teenagers to value education and strive for achievement, adults must behave as if doing well in school—not just finishing school, but actually doing well in school—is more important than socializing, more important than organized sports, more important than working at after-school jobs—more important than any other activity in which young people are involved. Although the problems of inner-city schools surely deserve our attention, the public needs to know that the problem of low student engagement is pervasive across affluent as well as disadvantaged communities.

3. INCREASE PARENTAL EFFECTIVENESS

We must have a serious and open discussion about the high rate of parental irresponsibility in this country and the toll it is taking on youngsters' lives. The widespread disengagement of parents from the business of child-rearing is a public health problem that warrants urgent national attention.

We now know enough about the fundamentals of good parenting to mount a systematic effort to educate parents in the most effective socialization techniques. We also know that parenting skills can be taught through well-designed programs. It is imperative that we translate this knowledge into action, by teaching parents how to be more effective in raising their children—not just in infancy, but throughout childhood and adolescence. This can be accomplished through community-based parent education programs, school-sponsored "clinics" for parents, and public service programming aimed at improving the quality of family life and parent-child relationships.

4. INCREASE PARENTAL INVOLVEMENT IN SCHOOL

A shockingly low percentage of American parents are involved in their children's education in any meaningful way. Merely asking parents to help monitor their children's homework assignments and course selection—what constitutes parent involvement in most school districts today—is not sufficient. Schools must expand efforts to actively draw parents into school programs. This will require restructuring and rescheduling school programs to meet the needs of working parents.

5. MAKE SCHOOL PERFORMANCE REALLY COUNT

There probably is little we can do to alter the adolescent peer culture directly, but we must recognize that the prevailing and pervasive peer norm of "getting by" is in part a direct consequence of socializing students within an educational system that neither rewards excellence nor punishes failure. The vast majority of students know all too well that the grades they earn in school will, under the present system, have little or no impact on their future educational or occupational success.

Although schools have played a role in creating this situation, they have been duly assisted by parents, employers, and institutions of higher education. In our study, more than half of all students say they could bring home grades of C or worse without their parents getting upset, and one-quarter say they could bring home grades of D or worse without it bothering their parents. Few employers ask to see students' high school or college transcripts. With the exception of our country's most selective colleges and universities, our postsecondary educational institutions are willing to accept virtually any applicant with a high school diploma, regardless of his or her scholastic record. This must be changed.

6. ADOPT A SYSTEM OF NATIONAL STANDARDS AND EXAMINATIONS

As many other commentators on American education have suggested, we should adopt a system of minimum national standards and performance-based examinations for promotion and graduation within American schools. Individual districts might be free to set higher standards than those mandated, but all should be expected to comply with the national minimums. Rather than reiterate the specifics of many good proposals on how we might go about doing this, I refer readers to Diane Ravitch's excellent book, *National Standards in American Education*.

In view of the pattern of ethnic differences in achievement uncovered in our research, it is fair to ask whether the implementation of a system of national standards and examinations will differentially affect students from different ethnic backgrounds. That is, given the fact that African-American and Latino students—and, especially, those from low-income families—currently lag behind their peers in school achievement, won't a system of national standards and examinations expose disproportionate numbers of these students to the risk of being held back in school?

There is no question that if a system of demanding national standards were implemented today, some students who would otherwise have been passed through the educational system without demonstrating scholastic competence would not be promoted and would require additional years of schooling before being able to qualify for a high school diploma or being eligible to apply for college admission. And, given the data on ethnic differences in achievement (both in terms of school grades and performance on standardized achievement tests), it is likely that, in the short term, relatively more of these students will be Black or Latino. This, understandably, has been an argument against using national standards to determine academic progress.

Whether a system of national standards and examinations will disproportionately harm Black and Latino students *in the long run* is a different matter, however. The answer depends on our willingness to shed the time-honored American belief that school achievement is determined by native ability and that some groups of students are inherently more able than others. Too many American students—and far too many Black and Latino students—have been short-changed by an educational system that has been willing to lower its standards in order to protect students from academic failure. The protection these students have been afforded, however, has resulted in their being placed in classes for less able students, where they receive a low-quality education, meaningless credentials, and, most horribly, inadequate preparation for further schooling or high-paying work.

If there is a lesson we can learn from Japanese educators, it is not to be found by studying the ways in which they structure their school year, train their teachers, or organize their classroom activities. What we ought to borrow from the Japanese—and communicate to every student and parent in this country—is the belief that success in school comes from hard work, not native intelligence, and that all children, if they are given instruction that is not only supportive, but appropriately demanding, can learn what they need to know to be educated and competent members of society. As Ravitch puts it, "If more is expected of children, they will stretch to meet those expectations." To this wise assessment I would only add that if more is expected of children in school, their *parents'* efforts will expand as well.

7. DEVELOP UNIFORM NATIONAL STANDARDS FOR SCHOOL TRANSCRIPTS

One reason that actual school performance matters so little is that we have no standardized way of communicating information about a student's academic accomplishments to parents, employers, and educators. Standardized aptitude tests, like the SAT, do not convey information about what a student has actually learned in school or about the specific competencies a student has or lacks. Standardized school transcripts should be developed that provide information about student performance on national achievement examinations, courses completed (with some indication of course difficulty), grades earned, and other indicators of scholastic motivation, such as school attendance.

8. ELIMINATE REMEDIAL EDUCATION AT FOUR-YEAR COLLEGES AND UNIVERSITIES

The current practice of providing remedial education in such basic academic skills as reading, writing, and mathematics to entering college students is disastrous. It has trivialized the significance of the high school diploma, diminished the meaning of college admission, eroded the value of a college degree, and drained precious resources away from bona fide college-level instruction.

I realize that despite whatever national standards and exams are put into place at the elementary and secondary school levels, there will be students who pass through the system without some of the requisite academic skills. But these students should not be entering four-year colleges and universities. Rather, students who have managed to complete high school but who lack the necessary college entry skills should be required to pursue remedial coursework at local community and two-year colleges before they can apply for admission to more advanced institutions of higher education.

9. SUPPORT APPROPRIATE SCHOOL-SPONSORED EXTRACURRICULAR ACTIVITIES

In modest amounts, participation in school-sponsored extracurricular activities strengthens youngsters' commitment to school and carries benefits that spill over into the classroom. This seems especially the case for less academically talented students. For this reason, schools should continue to support extracurricular activities and attempt to involve as many students as possible in them. An extensive extracurricular program is beneficial to the school, to the community, and to students. Rather than prohibit extracurricular participation among students with poor academic records, schools should attempt to remedy the academic problems of such students while permitting them to continue to participate.

It is nevertheless important to bear in mind that when a student's participation in extracurricular activities exceeds 20 hours weekly, the costs of participating begin to outweigh the benefits. Schools should therefore reexamine their extracurricular programs to ensure that they do not tax students' time and energy unnecessarily. Athletic programs, particularly football and basketball, warrant special scrutiny, since these are activities that tend to be the most time-consuming.

10. LIMIT YOUNGSTERS' TIME IN AFTER-SCHOOL JOBS

Heavy commitment to a part-time job during the school year significantly interferes with youngsters' school achievement and scholastic commitment. Students who are employed for more than 20 hours weekly perform worse in school, are less committed to their education, and are less engaged in class than their classmates who work less or not at all. Extensive employment is also linked to higher rates of teenage drug and alcohol use.

Ultimately, I believe that parents must decide whether and how much their children should be working. But not all parents are aware of the dangers of excessive employment, and current child labor regulations permit students to work far more during the school year than is good for their scholastic development or psychological well-being. As of this writing, twenty-nine states have *no* limits at all on the numbers of hours that students who are sixteen and older may work each week during the school year, and an additional thirteen states permit 40 or more hours of employment per week. Of eight states that have more stringent restrictions on weekly hours of employment during the school year, only two—Maine and Washington—limit school-year employment to 20 hours weekly or less.

We must reconsider the proposition that after-school employment is inherently beneficial for teenagers in light of the changing nature of the labor force and the increased demand for high-skilled, highly educated workers. There is very little evidence that students learn the sorts of skills and competencies they will need to be successful adult workers from the after-school jobs that are widely available, while there is considerable proof that extensive after-school employment has more costs than benefits.

. . .

For far too long, our national debate about the declining achievement of our students has been dominated by disputes over how schools ought to be changed without simultaneously examining the other forces in students' lives that affect their willingness to learn and their ability to achieve. It is time to leave behind the myopic view that schools determine student achievement, that the reasons for the achievement decline inhere in changed educational policies and practices, that deficiencies in our schools are the cause of our poor showing in international competitions, and, most importantly, that school reform—whether liberal or conservative in its orientation—is the solution to America's achievement problem.

No curricular overhaul, no instructional innovation, no change in school organization, no toughening of standards, no rethinking of teacher training or compensation will succeed if students do not come to school interested in, and committed to, learning. In order to understand how this commitment develops, why it has waned over the past three decades, and, more importantly, how we can reengage students in the business of learning, we need to look, not at what goes on inside the classroom, but at students' lives outside the school's walls. Until we do just this, school reform will continue to be a disappointment, and our students' achievement will fail to improve.

Appendix

OVERVIEW OF THE RESEARCH DESIGN

POPULATION

Our sample came from the student bodies of nine high schools in Wisconsin and Northern California. The schools were selected to yield a sample of students from different socioeconomic brackets, a variety of ethnic backgrounds (African-, Asian-, European-, and Hispanic-American), different family structures (e.g., intact, divorced, and remarried), and different types of communities (urban, suburban, and rural). Data were collected during the 1987–88, 1988–89, and 1989–90 school years.

We spent considerable energy before the study began in building strong relationships with the participating schools, so that the school administrators and teachers understood the purposes of our study and saw its potential significance. (Actually, we were approached by more schools who wanted to be included in the research than we could financially afford to include—surely a sign that what we were studying was viewed by administrators and teachers as important.) Because of the schools' cooperation, the study went relatively smoothly at each site.

PROCEDURE

All parents in the participating schools were informed, by First Class mail, of the date and nature of our study well in advance of the administering of the scheduled questionnaire. (We provided schools with letters in stamped, unaddressed envelopes to be mailed by school officials in order to protect the privacy of the families.) Parents were asked to call or write to their child's school or our research office if they did not want their child to participate in the study. Fewer than 1 percent of the adolescents in each of the target schools had their participation withheld by their parents.

All of the students in atttendance on each day of testing were invited to participate in the study and asked to complete the questionnaires. Informed consent was obtained from all participating students. For each questionnaire administration, out of the total school populations, approximately 5 percent of the students chose not to participate (or had their participation withheld by parents), approximately 15 percent were absent from school on the day of questionnaire administration (this figure is comparable to national figures on daily school attendance), and approximately 80 percent provided complete questionnaires. Each year, approximately 12,000 students participated in the study. We also supplemented these surveys with focused interviews with groups of students in each school; one-on-one interviews with a sample of 600 high-, medium-, and low-achieving students from six of our schools; and one-on-one interviews with about 500 students' parents.

The study sample was evenly divided among males and females and among ninth-, tenth-, eleventh-, and twelfth-graders. The sample was quite diverse with respect to other demographic variables: more than 40 percent of the respondents were from an ethnic minority group; nearly one-third were from single-parent households or stepfamilies; and nearly one-third came from homes in which the parents have not attended school beyond the twelfth grade.

MEASURES

Adolescent adjustment, achievement, and behavior. Various indicators of adolescent adjustment, achievement, and behavior were measured via self-report surveys administered to the students. Generally, four sets of outcome variables were examined at various points in the research: psychosocial development, academic competence, internalized distress, and problem behavior. In virtually all cases, we used standardized measures that had been employed in previous research.

In social science research, investigators must worry about the honesty of their respondents. Although one can never be absolutely certain that individuals are telling the truth when they are completing questionnaires, there are several steps that a researcher can take to maximize honest responses, and several procedures one can employ to check to see if individuals are responding genuinely and openly.

When all of the questionnaires were completed, we checked each one for patterns of inconsistent or random responding that might indicate that a student had not completed the survey in good faith. If a questionnaire looked at all suspicious, it was not forwarded to our data processor for computer scanning. After the questionnaires were scanned, and the data entered into the computer, we once again checked to make sure that the answers each student provided were relatively consistent and logical. Because we occasionally asked the same question in slightly different ways within each questionnaire, we could compare students' responses to similar items and pull from the data file any questionnaires whose answers appeared unreliable.

We also checked to make sure that students accurately reported information on one of our most important variables—their grades in school—by comparing, in a separate study, a large subsample of students' reports of their grades to information we were able to obtain from the students' official school records. Although one might suspect that students would overstate their grades, our analysis showed that this was true only in a limited sense—not surprisingly, students whose grade-point average was lower than a C tended to inflate their grades somewhat. Overall, however, the correlation between students' own reports and the grades in the school records was remarkably high. Other studies that have followed similar procedures find that under conditions of confidentiality and anonymity, adolescents generally provide accurate information about their behavior and their relationships with parents and friends.

Parenting practices. Our battery concerning family relations is aimed primarily at understanding authoritative parenting and its impact on youngsters' development. "Authoritative parenting" is a term coined by Diana Baumrind to describe a constellation of parenting practices, values, and beliefs that combines warmth, acceptance, and involvement with structure, maturity demands, and firm behavioral control. The family relations questionnaire we developed contained many items on parenting practices that were taken or adapted from existing measures.

The use of adolescents' reports about their parents is justified on several grounds. Given the size of the sample, it was necessary to rely on questionnaire data, and the difficulties in obtaining data from disengaged parents in particular have already been mentioned. As well, parental self-reports tend to exaggerate both their acceptance and firmness and have been criticized as unreliable. Adolescents, on the other hand, are able to act as knowledgeable informants about parental behaviors. Moreover, some writers have argued that children's perceptions of their parents' behavior may be as important influences on their development as are parents' actual behaviors.

We supplemented the questionnaire-derived data on family relationships with face-to-face interviews with a sample of approximately 600 students (selected on the basis of ethnicity and academic performance) and their parents. Interviews with students were conducted at the student's school. Interviews with parents were conducted at home.

Peer crowds. Our chief index of peer association was based on the adolescent's membership within a peer crowd. Crowd affiliation was based on the Social Type Rating (STR) procedure, an efficient mechanism for identifying adolescents' peer group affiliation, based on their reputation among peers. Derived from earlier studies of adolescent peer groups, the STR procedure was a two-step process. In the first step, school administrators were asked to identify a set of boys and girls (within each ethnic group in multiethnic schools) in each grade who represented a good cross section of the school's student body. These students were interviewed in small groups composed of students of the same gender, same grade level, and same ethnic group. Through group discussion, each group derived a list of the school's major crowds; then each participant listed two boys and two girls in their grade who were the leaders or most prominent members of each crowd. From these lists, a stratified sample was drawn in each grade (stratified by crowd type, gender, and ethnicity, but with preference given to the most frequently listed students) to become "STR raters" in the second step.

Each rater, accompanied by a friend of her or his own choosing, was individually interviewed. The raters were presented with the list of crowds derived from the earlier group interviews, then asked to place each student in their grade level into one of the crowds. Raters could indicate that they did not know a student well enough to assign to a crowd. STR ratings continued until each student had been rated by at least ten STR raters. Because raters could only deal with about three hundred names in the time allotted for STR interviews, class lists in the larger schools were partitioned and the number of raters increased to ensure that all students received the required number of ratings.

Once STR interviews were completed, crowd ratings for each student were collated and analyzed. A student was assigned to a crowd if at least 50 percent of STR raters knew the student well enough to classify him or her into a crowd and if over 50 percent of the raters who did classify the student concurred on the student's crowd affiliation. To increase the generalizability of results and our ability to compare findings to previous ethnographic research on adolescent peer groups, we restricted analyses to students associated with one of six crowd types: *jocks, populars, brains, druggies, loners,* and *normals.*

Social network. We were also interested in the influence of the individuals in the adolescent's immediate social network. Subjects were asked to provide the names of up to five of their closest friends from school. Because these friends also were participants in the study, we were able to match data on parenting practices or adjustment outcomes provided by each respondent with those provided by each of his or her friends. For questions in which we were interested in characterizing peer networks, we limited our analyses to respondents who nominated at least three friends who provided complete information on the variables in question.

Neighborhood. We know the street addresses of approximately 75 percent of the youngsters in our sample and have used this information to investigate neighborhood effects. In the absence of clear guidelines as to what constitutes a neighborhood, however, we explored these effects at different levels of analysis. In some, we grouped youngsters together by U.S. Census tract. In others, we coded our respondents' addresses into real neighborhoods, defined not by the Census, but by residents familiar with the community. In some areas, for example, we obtained maps used by city planning offices, realtors, or school districts. These maps provide a breakdown of geographical areas into neighborhoods defined by residents' perceptions and historic, if occasionally unusual, boundaries. Using these maps, we were able to cluster respondents in our sample into neighborhoods on the basis of their street addresses.

PREVIOUSLY PUBLISHED REPORTS

Some of the findings contained in this book were reported previously in chapters prepared for scholarly outlets and in presentations at professional meetings of psychologists, sociologists, and educators. These articles contain technical details about the research design and data analysis. Among the most important of these publications are:

Bogenschneider, K., and Steinberg, L. "Maternal Employment and Adolescent Academic Achievement: A Developmental Analysis." *Sociology of Education* 67 (1994): 60–77.

Brown, B., et al. "Parenting Practices and Peer Group Affiliation in Adolescence." *Child Development* 64 (1993): 467–82.

Darling, N., and Steinberg, L. "Community Influences on Adolescent Achievement and Deviance." In G. Duncan, J. Brooks-Gunn, and L. Aber, eds., *Community Influences on Child and Adolescent Development.* New York: Russell Sage Foundation, in press.

Darling, N., and Steinberg L. "Parenting Style as Context: An Integrative Model." *Psychological Bulletin* 113 (1993): 487–96.

Darling, N., Steinberg, L., and Gringlas, M. "Community Influences on Adolescent Achievement and Deviance: A Test of the Functional Community Hypothesis." Under review by *Child Development.*

Dornbusch, S. "Off the Track." Presidential address at the biennial meeting of the Society for Research on Adolescence, San Diego, February 1994.

Dornbusch, S., Ritter, P., and Steinberg, L. "Differences Between African Americans and Non-Hispanic Whites in the Relation of Family Statuses to Adolescent School Performance." *American Journal of Education,* August 1991, 543–67.

Dornbusch, S. M., et al. "Family Decision-making and Academic Performance in a Diverse High School Population." *Journal of Adolescent Research* 5(2)(1990): 143–60.

Dornbusch, S. M., et al. "The Relation of Parenting Style to Adolescent School Performance." *Child Development* 58 (1987): 1244–57.

Dornbusch, S., et al. "Stressful Events and Their Correlates Among Adolescents of Diverse Backgrounds." In M. Colten and S. Gore, eds., *Adolescent Stress: Causes and Consequences,* 111–30. Hawthorne, N.Y.: Aldine de Gruyter, 1991.

Fletcher, A., Darling, N., and Steinberg, L. "Parenting Practices as Moderators of Peer Influence on Adolescent Deviance." In J. McCord, ed., *Coercion and Punishment in Long-term Perspectives.* New York: Cambridge University Press, 1995.

Fletcher, A., et al. "The Company They Keep: Relation of Adolescents' Adjustment and Behavior to Their Friends' Perceptions of Authoriative Parenting in the Social Network." *Development Psychology* 31 (1995): 300–310.

Glasgow, K., et al. "Parenting Styles, Dysfunctional Attributions, and Adolescent Outcomes in Diverse Groups." Under review by *Child Development.*

Lamborn, S., Dornbusch, S., and Steinberg, L. "Ethnicity and Community Context as Moderators of the Relation Between Family Decision-making and Adolescent Adjustment." *Child Development,* in press.

Lamborn, S., et al. "Patterns of Competence and Adjustment Among Adolescents from Authoritative, Authoritarian, Indulgent, and Neglectful Homes." *Child Development* 62 (1991): 1049–65.

Mounts, N., and Steinberg, L. "Peer Influences on Adolescent Achievement and Deviance: An Ecological Approach." *Development Psychology* 31 (1995), 915–22.

Steinberg, L., and Cauffman, B. "The Impact of School-Year Employment on Adolescent Development." In R. Vasta, ed., *Annals of Child Development,* vol. 11, 131–66. London: Jessica Kingsley Publishers, 1995.

Steinberg, L., and Dornbusch, S. "Negative Correlates of Part-time Work in Adolescence: Replication and Elaboration." *Developmental Psychology* 27 (1991): 304–13.

Steinberg, L., Dornbusch, S., and Brown, B. "Ethnic Differences in Adolescent Achievement: An Ecological Perspective." *American Psychologist* 47 (1992): 723–29.

Steinberg, L., Elmen, J., and Mounts, N. "Authoritative Parenting, Psychosocial Maturity, and Academic Success Among Adolescents." *Child Development* 60 (1989): 1424–36.

Steinberg, L., Fegley, S., and Dornbusch, S. "Negative Impact of Part-time Work on Adolescent Adjustment: Evidence from a Longitudinal Study." *Developmental Psychology* 29 (1993): 171–80.

Steinberg, L., Fletcher, A., and Darling, N. "Parental Monitoring and Peer Influences on Adolescent Substance Use." *Pediatrics* 93(6)(1994): 1060–64.

Steinberg, L., et al. "Authoritative Parenting and Adolescent Adjustment: An Ecological Journey." In P. Moen, G. Elder, Jr., and K. Luscher, eds., *Examining Lives in Context: Perspectives on the Ecology of Human Development,* 223–66. Washington, D.C.: American Psychological Association, 1995.

Steinberg, L., et al. "Authoritative Parenting and Adolescent Adjustment Across Various Ecological Niches." *Journal of Research on Adolescence* 1 (1990): 19–36.

Steinberg, L., et al. "Impact of Parenting Practices on Adolescent Achievement: Authoritative Parenting, School Involvement, and Encouragement to Succeed." *Child Development* 63 (1992): 1266–81.

Steinberg, L., et al. "Over-Time Changes in Adjustment and Competence Among Adolescents from Authoritative, Authoritarian, Indulgent, and Neglectful Families." *Child Development* 65 (1994): 754–70.

Notes

CHAPTER 1: THE REAL PROBLEM

PAGE

13 **consistently poor showing on standardized tests:** Diane Ravitch, *National Standards in American Education: A Citizen's Guide* (Washington, D.C.: Brookings Institution, 1995).

15 **our research team used the term** *engagement:* Fred Newmann, ed., *Student Engagement and Achievement in American Secondary Schools* (New York: Teachers College Press, 1992).

16 **competitiveness in the international marketplace** National Center on Education and the Economy, *America's Choice: High Skills or Low Wages!* (Washington, D.C.: National Center on Education and the Economy, 1990).

16 **Doing well in school:** David L. Featherman, "Schooling and Occupational Careers: Constancy and Change in Worldly Success," in O. Brim and J. Kagan, eds., *Constancy and Change in Human Development* (Cambridge: Harvard University Press, 1980), 675–738.

17 **psychological and behavioral problems:** Richard Jessor and Shirley Jessor, *Problem Behavior and Psychosocial Development: A Longitudinal Study of Youth* (New York: Academic Press, 1977).

CHAPTER 2: A NATION AT RISK, A NATION IN DENIAL

PAGE

31 **The decline in SAT scores:** Ravitch, *National Standards*.

31 **analyses of changes in SAT scores:** Charles Murray and Richard Herrnstein, "What's Really Behind the SAT-Score Decline?" *Public Interest* 106 (1992): 32–56.

32 **"The Nation's Report Card":** Ravitch, *National Standards*; see also *NAEP 1992 Trends in Academic Progress* (Washington, D.C.: U.S. Department of Education, 1994).

33 **"this does not mean":** Ravitch, *National Standards*, 67.

36 **the gap between our students' achievement:** Harold Stevenson and James Stigler, *The Learning Gap: Why Our Schools Are Failing and What We Can Learn from Japanese and Chinese Education* (New York: Simon & Schuster, 1992).

36 **1983 report:** National Commission on Excellence in Education, *A Nation at Risk: The Imperative for Educational Reform* (Washington, D.C.: U.S. Department of Education, 1983).

37 **"A close examination":** Stevenson and Stigler, *Learning Gap*, 50.

37 **"the 'best students' in the United States":** Ravitch, *National Standards*, 88.

38 **"If an unfriendly foreign power":** National Commission on Excellence in Education, *Nation at Risk*, 5.

38 **America will not be able to compete:** National Center on Education and the Economy, *America's Choice*.

40 **how poorly equipped our college graduates are:** P. Barton and A. Lapointe, *National Adult Literacy Study* (Princeton, N.J.: Educational Testing Service, 1994).

42 **"Americans persist in believing":** Stevenson and Stigler, *Learning Gap*, 29.

44 **the "glorification of stupidity":** *New York Times* columnist Bob Herbert made a similar observation: "In an era in which the ability to acquire and properly process information has become profoundly important, America insists on being, to a large extent, a nation of nitwits. Consider, for example, some of our recent top-grossing movies: 'The Brady Bunch Movie,' a ditzy reprise of a ditzy 1970's situation comedy about a terminally ditzy family; 'Dumb and Dumber,' which is even dumber than the title indicates; and 'Billy Madison,' a full-length made-for-morons motion picture about—what else?—a moron. . . . I turned on 'Beavis and Butt-head' the other night, and it was so much worse—so much more stupid—than

anything I had imagined that I just sat staring in astonishment. . . . None of this would be important if we were talking only about fads, goofy things that make a momentary appearance, spark a chuckle and pass harmlessly from sight. But that is not what is going on. We are surrounded by a deep and abiding stupidity" (*The New York Times*, March 1, 1995).

46 **"overall drop in achievement":** Daniel Koretz, *Trends in Educational Achievement* (Washington, D.C.: Congressional Budget Office, 1986), 53.

CHAPTER 3: SCHOOL REFORM IS NOT THE SOLUTION

PAGE

50 **young adolescents in London schools:** Michael Rutter et al. *Fifteen Thousand Hours: Secondary Schools and Their Effects on Children* (London: Open Books, 1979).

51 **the United States spends far more:** Stevenson and Stigler, *Learning Gap.*

53 **in order to provide adequate opportunities:** For example, see Joy Dryfoos, "Schools as Places for Health, Mental Health, and Social Services," *Teachers College Record* 94 (1993): 540–67.

53 **more than one-quarter of all American young people:** National Research Council, *Losing Generations* (Washington, D.C.: National Academy Press, 1993).

55 **the proportion of school budgets:** Stevenson and Stigler, *Learning Gap.*

55 **Only 40 percent of students' school days:** National Education Commission on Time and Learning, *Prisoners of Time* (Washington, D.C.: U.S. Government Printing Office, 1994).

59 **The links between IQ and school performance:** Featherman, "Schooling."

59 **far more influenced by environmental factors:** L. Thompson, D. Detterman, and R. Plomin, "Associations Between Cognitive Abilities and Scholastic Achievement: Genetic Overlap but Environmental Differences," *Psychological Science* 2 (1991):158–65.

CHAPTER 4: DISENGAGED STUDENTS

PAGE

65 **the average intelligence of the population:** Richard Herrnstein and Charles Murray, *The Bell Curve: Intelligence and Class Structure in American Life* (New York: Free Press, 1994).

68 **the majority of high school students:** Andrew Fuligni and Harold Stevenson, "Time-Use and Academic Achievement Among American, Chinese, and Japanese High School Students," *Child Development*, in press.

69 **teacher expectations and student employment:** Linda McNeil, *Lowering Expectations: The Impact of Student Employment on Classroom Knowledge* (Madison: Wisconsin Center for Educational Research, 1984), 5.

CHAPTER 5: ETHNICITY AND ADOLESCENT ACHIEVEMENT

PAGE

78 **about one-third of the adolescent population:** James Wetzel, *American Youth: A Statistical Snapshot* (New York: William T. Grant Foundation Commission on Work, Family, and Citizenship, 1987).

82 **The ethnic differences in achievement:** See, for example, Roslyn Mickelson, "The Attitude-Achievement Paradox Among Black Adolescents," *Sociology of Education* 63 (1990): 44–61; Stanley Sue and Sumie Okazaki, "Asian-American Educational Achievement: A Phenomenon in Search of an Explanation," *American Psychologist* 45 (1990): 913–20.

83 **ethnic group comparisons of achievement:** For example, see Karen Bogenschneider and Laurence Steinberg, "Maternal Employment and Adolescent Academic Achievement: A Developmental Analysis," *Sociology of Education* 67 (1994): 60–77.

87 **studies directly examining the genetic explanation:** Sue and Okazaki, "Asian-American Educational Achievement."

88 **Indochinese refugee families.** See Nathan Caplan et al., *The Boat People and Achievement in America: A Study of Family Life, Hard Work, and Cultural Values* (Ann Arbor: University of Michigan Press, 1989); N. Caplan, M. Choy, and J. Whitmore, "Indochinese Refugee Families and Academic Achievement," *Scientific American*, February 1992, 36–42.

89 **students tend to be assigned to tracks:** Karl Alexander and Michael Cook, "Curricula and Coursework: A Surprise Ending to a Familiar Story," *American Sociological Review* 47 (1982): 626–40; Sanford Dornbusch, "Off the Track" (presidential address at the biennial meeting of the Society for Research on Adolescence, San Diego, February 1994).

90 **ethnic differences in students' beliefs:** John Ogbu, "Variability in Minority School Performance: A Problem in Search of an Explanation," *Anthropology and Education Quarterly* 18 (1987): 312–34.

91 **students' achievement attributions:** Valerie Henderson and Carol Dweck,

"Motivation and Achievement," in S. Feldman and G. Elliott, eds., *At the Threshold: The Developing Adolescent* (Cambridge: Harvard University Press, 1990), 308–29.

92 **Americans are far more likely to believe:** Susan Holloway, "Concepts of Ability and Effort in Japan and the United States," *Review of Educational Research* 58 (1988): 327–45.

94 **the achievement gap:** Laurence Steinberg, "Why Japan's Students Outdo Ours," *The New York Times*, April 25, 1987.

94 **the adolescent suicide rate:** David Crystal et al., "Psychological Maladjustment and Academic Achievement: A Cross-Cultural Study of Japanese, Chinese, and American High School Students," *Child Development* 65 (1994): 738–53.

95 **minor signs of psychological distress:** Ibid.

96 **"Asian students' academic success":** Keunho Keefe and Sylvia Alva, *Asian-American Adolescents' School Success: Is It at the Expense of Social Costs?* (paper presented at the biennial meeting of the Society for Research in Child Development, Indianapolis, March 1995).

98 **becoming Americanized is detrimental to youngsters' achievement:** Grace Kao and Marta Tienda, "Optimism and Achievement: The Educational Performance of Immigrant Youth," *Social Science Quarterly*, in press.

CHAPTER 6: THE POWER OF AUTHORITATIVE PARENTING

PAGE

106 **three fundamental dimensions of parenting:** Earl Schaefer, "Children's Reports of Parental Behavior: An Inventory," *Child Development* 36 (1965): 413–24; Laurence Steinberg, "Autonomy, Conflict, and Harmony in the Family Relationship," in S. Feldman and G. Elliot, eds., *At the Threshold: The Developing Adolescent* (Cambridge: Harvard University Press, 1990), 255–76.

111 **parenting "styles":** Diana Baumrind, "Parental Disciplinary Patterns and Social Competence in Children," *Youth and Society* 9 (1978): 239–76; Nancy Darling and Laurence Steinberg, "Parenting Style as Context: An Integrative Model," *Psychological Bulletin* 113 (1993): 487–96.

114 **authoritative parenting is superior:** Eleanor Maccoby and John Martin, "Socialization in the Context of the Family: Parent-Child Interaction," in E. M. Hetherington, ed., *Handbook of Child Psychology*, vol. 4, *Socialization, Personality, and Social Development* (New York: Wiley, 1983), 1–101.

119 **MetLife survey.** Metropolitan Life Survey of the American Teacher, *Violence in America's Public Schools: The Family Perspective* (New York: MetLife, 1994).

CHAPTER 7: THE HOME ENVIRONMENT
OF ACADEMICALLY SUCCESSFUL STUDENTS

PAGE

125 **parental involvement works:** Wendy Grolnick and Marcia Slowiaczek, "Parents' Involvement in Children's Schooling: A Multidimensional Conceptualization and Motivational Model," *Child Development* 64 (1994): 237–52; David Stevenson and David Baker, "The Family-School Relation and the Child's School Performance," *Child Development* 58 (1987): 1348–57.

126 **parents of successful students:** See also Annette Lareau, *Home Advantage: Social Class and Parental Intervention in Elementary Education* (New York: Falmer Press, 1989).

129 **American parents' involvement:** Susan Chira, "Parents Take Less of a Role as Pupils Age," *The New York Times*, September 5, 1994.

129 **drop-off in parental involvement:** Stevenson and Stigler, *Learning Gap*.

CHAPTER 8: THE POWER OF PEERS

PAGE

139 **The adolescent's social world:** B. Bradford Brown, "Peer Groups," in S. Feldman and G. Elliott, eds., *At the Threshold: The Developing Adolescent* (Cambridge: Harvard University Press, 1990), 171–96.

141 **changes in individuals' susceptibility to peer pressure:** Laurence Steinberg and Susan Silverberg, "The Vicissitudes of Autonomy in Early Adolescence," *Child Development* 57 (1986): 841–51.

142 **Friends can influence each other's school performance:** Joyce L. Epstein, "The Influence of Friends on Achievement and Affective Outcomes," in J. Epstein and N. Karweit, eds., *Friends in School* (New York: Academic Press, 1983), 177–200.

143 **All schools have crowds:** Brown, "Peer Groups."

149 **three sets of forces:** B. Bradford Brown et al., "Parenting Practices and Peer Group Affiliation in Adolescence," *Child Development* 64 (1993): 467–82.

152 **how neighborhoods affect children's behavior:** Anne Fletcher et al., "The Company They Keep: Relation of Adolescents' Adjustment and Behavior to Their Friends' Perceptions of Authoritative Parenting in the Social Network," *Developmental Psychology* 31 (1995): 300–310; Nancy Darling and Laurence Steinberg, "Community Influences on Adolescent Achievement and Deviance," in G. Duncan, J. Brooks-Gunn, and L. Aber, eds., *Community Influences on Child and Adolescent Development* (New York: Russell Sage Foundation, in press).

158 **one of the few routes to social mobility:** Sue and Okazaki, "Asian-American Educational Achievement."

159 **students who tried to do well in school:** Signithia Fordham and John Ogbu, "Black Students' School Success: Coping with the Burden of 'Acting White,'" *Urban Review* 18 (1986): 176–206; see also Signithia Fordham, "Racelessness as a Factor in Black Students' School Success: Pragmatic Strategy or Pyrrhic Victory?" *Harvard Educational Review* 58 (1988): 54–84.

160 **"[W]hite Americans traditionally refused":** Fordham and Ogbu, "Black Students' School Success," 177.

CHAPTER 9: ALL WORK AND ALL PLAY MAKES JACK A DUMB BOY

PAGE

165 **The widespread employment of American high school students:** See Laurence Steinberg and Elizabeth Cauffman, "The Impact of School-Year Employment on Adolescent Development," in R. Vasta, ed., *Annals of Child Development*, vol. 11 (London: Jessica Kingsley Publishers, 1995), 131–66; Ellen Greenberger and Laurence Steinberg, *When Teenagers Work: The Psychological and Social Costs of Adolescent Employment* (New York: Basic Books, 1986).

171 **working teenagers get less rest.** Mary Carskadon, Mancuso, J., and Rosekind, M., "Impact of Part-time Employment on Adolescent Sleep Patterns," *Sleep Research* 18 (1989): 114.

172 **The United States is the only country:** Greenberger and Steinberg, *When Teenagers Work*.

174 **participation in various extracurricular activities:** Data from Laura Berk, "The Extracurriculum," in P. Jackson, ed., *Handbook of Research on Curriculum* (New York: Macmillan, 1992).

177 **time spent "playing":** Fuligni and Stevenson, "Time Use and Academic Achievement"; Stevenson and Stigler, *Learning Gap*.

179 **socializing with friends was a stronger predictor:** Fuligni and Stevenson, "Time Use and Academic Achievement."

179 **international differences in parents' values:** Andrew Fuligni, "Academic Achievement and Motivation Among Asian-American and European-American Early Adolescents" (paper presented at the biennial meeting of the Society for Research on Adolescence, San Diego, February 1994); Stevenson and Stigler, *Learning Gap*.

CHAPTER 10: BEYOND THE CLASSROOM

PAGE

191 **"If more is expected":** Ravitch, *National Standards*, 180.

Bibliography

Alexander, K., and Cook, M. "Curricula and Coursework: A Surprise Ending to a Familiar Story." *American Sociological Review* 47 (1982): 626–40.

Barton, P., and Lapointe, A. *National Adult Literacy Survey.* Princeton, N.J.: Educational Testing Service, 1994.

Baumrind, D. "Parental Disciplinary Patterns and Social Competence in Children." *Youth and Society* 9 (1978): 239–76.

Berk, L. "The Extracurriculum." In P. Jackson, ed., *Handbook of Research on Curriculum.* New York: Macmillan, 1992.

Bogenschneider, K., and Steinberg, L. "Maternal Employment and Adolescent Academic Achievement: A Developmental Analysis." *Sociology of Education* 67 (1994): 60–77.

Brown, B. "Peer Groups." In S. Feldman and G. Elliott, eds., *At the Threshold: The Developing Adolescent,* 171–96. Cambridge: Harvard University Press, 1990.

Brown, B., et al. "Parenting Practices and Peer Group Affiliation in Adolescence." *Child Development* 64 (1993): 467–82.

Caplan, N., Choy, M., and Whitmore, J. "Indochinese Refugee Families and Academic Achievement." *Scientific American*, February 1992, 36–42.

Caplan, N., et al. *The Boat People and Achievement in America: A Study of Family Life, Hard Work, and Cultural Values.* Ann Arbor: University of Michigan Press, 1989.

Carskadon, M., Mancuso, J., and Rosekind, M. "Impact of Part-time Employment on Adolescent Sleep Patterns." *Sleep Research* 18 (1989): 114.

Chira, S. "Parents Take Less of a Role as Pupils Age." *The New York Times*, September 5, 1994.

Crystal, D., et al. "Psychological Maladjustment and Academic Achievement: A Cross-Cultural Study of Japanese, Chinese, and American High School Students." *Child Development* 65 (1994): 738–53.

Darling, N., and Steinberg, L. "Community Influences on Adolescent Achievement and Deviance." In G. Duncan, J. Brooks-Gunn, and L. Aber, eds., *Community Influences on Child and Adolescent Development*. New York: Russell Sage Foundation, in press.

Darling, N., and Steinberg, L. "Parenting Style as Context: An Integrative Model." *Psychological Bulletin* 113 (1993): 487–96.

Dornbusch, S. "Off the Track." Presidential address at the biennial meeting of the Society for Research on Adolescence, San Diego, February 1994.

Dornbusch, S. M., et al. "The Relation of Parenting Style to Adolescent School Performance." *Child Development* 58 (1987): 1244–57.

Dryfoos, J. "Schools as Places for Health, Mental Health, and Social Services." *Teachers College Record* 94 (1993): 540–67.

Epstein, J. L. "The Influence of Friends on Achievement and Affective Outcomes." In J. Epstein and N. Karweit, eds., *Friends in School*, 177–200. New York: Academic Press, 1983.

Featherman, D. "Schooling and Occupational Careers: Constancy and Change in Worldly Success." In O. Brim and J. Kagan, eds., *Constancy and Change in Human Development*, 675–738. Cambridge: Harvard University Press, 1980.

Fletcher, A., et al. "The Company They Keep: Relation of Adolescents' Adjustment and Behavior to Their Friends' Perceptions of Authoritative Parenting in the Social Network." *Developmental Psychology* 31 (1995): 300–310.

Fordham, S. "Racelessness as a Factor in Black Students' School Success: Pragmatic Strategy or Pyrrhic Victory?" *Harvard Educational Review* 58 (1988): 54–84.

Fordham, S., and Ogbu, J. U. "Black Students' School Success: Coping with the Burden of 'Acting White.'" *Urban Review* 18 (1986): 176–206.

Fuligni, A. "Academic Achievement and Motivation Among Asian-American and European-American Early Adolescents." Paper presented at the biennial meeting of the Society for Research on Adolescence, San Diego, February 1994.

Fuligni, A., and Stevenson, H. "Time-Use and Academic Achievement Among American, Chinese, and Japanese High School Students." *Child Development*, in press.

Greenberger, E., and Steinberg, L. *When Teenagers Work: The Psychological and Social Costs of Adolescent Employment*. New York: Basic Books, 1986.

Grolnick, W., and Slowiaczek, M. "Parents' Involvement in Children's Schooling: A Multidimensional Conceptualization and Motivational Model." *Child Development* 64 (1994): 237–52.

Henderson, V., and Dweck, C. "Motivation and Achievement." In S. Feldman and G. Elliott, eds., *At the Threshold: The Developing Adolescent*, 308–29. Cambridge: Harvard University Press, 1990.

Herbert, B. "A Nation of Nitwits." *The New York Times*, March 1, 1995.

Herrnstein, R., and Murray, C. *The Bell Curve: Intelligence and Class Structure in American Life*. New York: Free Press, 1994.

Holloway, S. "Concepts of Ability and Effort in Japan and the United States." *Review of Educational Research* 58 (1988): 327–45.

Jessor, R., and Jessor, S. *Problem Behavior and Psychosocial Development: A Longitudinal Study of Youth*. New York: Academic Press, 1977.

Kao, G., and Tienda, M. "Optimism and Achievement: The Educational Performance of Immigrant Youth." *Social Science Quarterly*, in press.

Keefe, K., and Alva, S. "Asian-American Adolescents' School Success: Is It at the Expense of Social Costs?" Paper presented at the biennial meeting of the Society for Research in Child Development, Indianapolis, March 1995.

Koretz, D. *Trends in Educational Achievement*. Washington, D.C.: Congressional Budget Office, 1986.

Lareau, A. *Home Advantage: Social Class and Parental Intervention in Elementary Education*. New York: Falmer Press, 1989.

Maccoby, E., and Martin, J. "Socialization in the Context of the Family: Parent-Child Interaction." In E. M. Hetherington, ed., *Handbook of Child Psychology*. Vol. 4, *Socialization, Personality, and Social Development*, 1–101. New York: Wiley, 1983.

McNeil, L. *Lowering Expectations: The Impact of Student Employment on Classroom Knowledge*. Madison: Wisconsin Center for Educational Research, 1984.

Metropolitan Life Survey of the American Teacher. *Violence in America's Public Schools: The Family Perspective*. New York: MetLife, 1994.

Mickelson, R. "The Attitude-Achievement Paradox Among Black Adolescents." *Sociology of Education* 63 (1990): 44–61.

Murray, C., and Herrnstein, R. "What's Really Behind the SAT-Score Decline?" *Public Interest* 106 (1992): 32–56.

NAEP 1992 Trends in Academic Progress. Washington, D.C.: U.S. Department of Education, 1994.

National Center on Education and the Economy. *America's Choice: High Skills or Low Wages!* Washington, D.C.: National Center on Education and the Economy, 1990.

National Commission on Excellence in Education. *A Nation at Risk: The Imperative for Educational Reform.* Washington, D.C.: U.S. Department of Education, 1983.

National Education Commission on Time and Learning. *Prisoners of Time.* Washington, D.C.: U.S. Government Printing Office, 1994.

National Research Council. *Losing Generations.* Washington, D.C.: National Academy Press, 1993.

Newmann, F., ed. *Student Engagement and Achievement in American Secondary Schools.* New York: Teachers College Press, 1992.

Ogbu, J. "Variability in Minority School Performance: A Problem in Search of an Explanation." *Anthropology and Education Quarterly* 18 (1987): 312–34.

Ravitch, D. *National Standards in American Education: A Citizen's Guide.* Washington, D.C.: Brookings Institution, 1995.

Rutter, M., et al.: *Fifteen Thousand Hours: Secondary Schools and Their Effects on Children.* London: Open Books, 1979.

Schaefer, E. "Children's Reports of Parental Behavior: An Inventory." *Child Development* 36 (1965): 413–24.

Steinberg, L. "Autonomy, Conflict, and Harmony in the Family Relationship." In S. Feldman and G. Elliot, eds., *At the Threshold: The Developing Adolescent,* 255–76. Cambridge: Harvard University Press, 1990.

Steinberg, L. "Why Japan's Students Outdo Ours." *The New York Times,* April 25, 1987.

Steinberg, L., and Cauffman, B. "The Impact of School-Year Employment on Adolescent Development." In R. Vasta, ed., *Annals of Child Development,* vol. 11, 131–66. London: Jessica Kingsley Publishers, 1995.

Steinberg, L., and Silverberg, S. "The Vicissitudes of Autonomy in Early Adolescence." *Child Development* 57 (1986): 841–51.

Stevenson, D., and Baker, D. "The Family-School Relation and the Child's School Performance." *Child Development* 58 (1987): 1348–57.

Stevenson, H., and Stigler, J. *The Learning Gap: Why Our Schools Are Failing and*

What We Can Learn from Japanese and Chinese Education. New York: Simon & Schuster, 1992.

Sue, S., and Okazaki, S. "Asian-American Educational Achievement: A Phenomenon in Search of an Explanation." *American Psychologist* 45 (1990): 913–20.

Thompson, L., Detterman, D., and Plomin, R. "Associations Between Cognitive Abilities and Scholastic Achievement: Genetic Overlap but Environmental Differences." *Psychological Science* 2 (1991): 158–65.

Wetzel, J. *American Youth: A Statistical Snapshot.* New York: William T. Grant Foundation Commission on Work, Family, and Citizenship, 1987.

INDEX

ability, engagement compared with, 64–66
acceptance vs. rejection, by parents, 106–7, 108–11, 112
achievement, *see* school achievement
achievement attribution, 91–94, 98, 124
acting out, 109
"acting White," 159–60
adolescents:
  after-school jobs of, *see* employment, after-school
  engagement of, *see* disengagement; engagement
  ethnicity and, *see* ethnicity
  as focus of student commitment study, 17–18
  home environment of, *see* authoritative parenting; parenting; parents
  increased troubles of, 62–63
  media portrayals of, 12–13, 62
  minorities as percentage of, 78
  society of, 143–45, 151–52
  susceptibility to peer pressure of, 140–43; *see also* peers; socializing
African-Americans, *see* Blacks

after-school employment, *see* employment, after-school
alcohol, 17, 26, 63, 96, 116, 121, 187
  after-school employment and, 171
  peer influence and, 148, 150–51
American Indians, 80
Americanization:
  Asian-Americans and, 98
  and ethnicity, 96–100
  immigrants and, 96–100
  Latinos and, 98, 185
  school achievement and, 96–100, 185
apprenticeship programs, 172
Asia, 36, 172, 173, 178, 180
Asian-Americans:
  achievement attribution and, 92
  Americanization and, 98
  consequences of failing as perceived by, 90–91
  engagement of, 86–87, 101, 186–87
  extracurricular activities and, 180–181
  high school achievement of, 79, 82–85, 87–91, 99–100, 131, 155–158, 181, 185, 187
  limited peer group access of, 157–158

Asian-Americans (*cont.*)
  parenting styles and, 133, 134, 135,
    136, 155–56
  from refugee families, 88
  in student commitment study, 21, 78,
    80
  suicide rates and, 94–95
  varied geographic and cultural back-
    grounds of, 80
athletics, *see* sports activities
attendance, class, 67, 87, 185
attribution style, 91–94, 98, 124
authoritarian (autocratic) parenting,
    112–14, 116–17, 120
authoritative (responsive) parenting:
  child development and, 114–15
  child's maturity as goal in, 113–14,
    123–24
  definition of, 112
  ethnicity and, 133–37
  psychological effects of, 116–18,
    123–24
  school achievement and, 122–23,
    126–27, 133
  school involvement and, 124–26
  social class and, 153
autocratic (authoritarian) parenting,
    112–14, 116–17, 120
autonomy vs. control, from parents, 106,
    107–11, 112–13

"back to basics," 48, 54, 55
  see also conservatives, school reform ap-
    proach of
"Beavis and Butt-head," 44
Bell Curve, The (Murray and Herrnstein),
    94
best friends, 139, 140
Billy Madison, 44
Blacks:
  achievement attribution and, 92
  "acting White" and, 159–60
  consequences of failing as perceived by,
    90–91
  low school achievement of, 79, 82–85,
    87–91, 131, 155–62, 185, 190–91
  media portrayals of, 160

parenting styles and, 133, 134, 135,
    136–37, 156
  in student commitment study, 21, 78,
    80
"book" learning, "hands-on" learning vs.,
    173
"brains," 19, 27, 144, 145, 158, 161
"breakdown" of family, 13, 24
"burnouts," 144
Bush, George, 47
busing, 21

California, 20, 84
Canada, 172
cheating, 18, 67
child labor laws, 166, 167, 193
China, People's Republic of, 36, 51
class attendance, 67, 87, 185
class difference, 21
  after-school employment and, 167
  NAEP data and, 34–35, 52
  parenting style and, 153
  school achievement and, 79, 81, 83,
    86
classes, students' choice of, 118–19
Clinton, Bill, 47
cliques, 139, 140
college-level, definition of, 38
commitment, *see* disengagement; engage-
    ment; student commitment study
community colleges, 38, 192
competence, social, 109, 114, 116, 117,
    120, 144
Congressional Budget Office, 46
conservatives, school reform approach of,
    48, 54–57, 69, 194
control vs. autonomy, from parents, 106,
    107–11, 112–13
crime, 17
crowds, peer, 139–41
cultural relativity, 132–33
curfew violations, 113–14
curricula, 48, 55–56

delinquency, 17, 26, 63, 95, 98, 116, 120,
    121, 145, 147–48, 187
Derry Township School Board, 11–12

disengagement, 61, 62–77
  behavior and, 66–69
  beliefs behind, 72–77
  consequences of, 28, 63
  definition of, 15
  emotions of, 70–72
  growth of, 28, 64
  motivation and, 72–74
  parental, 19–20, 118–21, 133, 134n, 137, 142, 153, 187
  psychological problems indicated by, 17
  see also engagement
divorce, 21–22, 115
  grades and, 86
dropping out, 171
"druggies," 19, 27, 144, 145
drugs, 13, 17, 26, 63, 96, 98, 116, 120, 187
  after-school employment and, 171
  peer influence and, 145, 148, 150–151
Dumb and Dumber, 44

economic costs of underachievement, 37–41
Educational Testing Service (ETS), 42, 43, 44
Education Department, U.S., 37
education spending, 48, 51–53, 54–55
effective parenting, 132–33, 189
employment, after-school, 18, 24, 163–73, 188–89
  behavioral effects of, 171
  ethnicity and, 180
  international comparisons of, 163–64, 172–73
  need for reduction in, 166–69
  number of students engaged in, 25, 164–66
  purchases made with earnings from, 167–68
  school achievement affected by, 19, 25, 69, 169–71
  social class and, 167
  time spent in, 19, 25, 68, 164, 168–71, 193

engagement, 61, 62–77
  ability compared with, 64–66
  of Asian-American students, 86–87, 101, 186–87
  behavior and, 66–69
  definition of, 15
  emotions of, 70–72
  importance of, 66
  social values indicated by, 16–17
  three suggestions for improvement of, 76–77
  see also disengagement
ethnicity:
  achievement attribution and, 91–94
  after-school employment and, 180
  Americanization and, 96–100
  cultural relativity and, 132–33
  definition and classification system of, 79–82
  extracurricular activities and, 180–182
  homework and, 87, 156, 185
  parenting styles and, 131–37
  peer groups and, 144, 155–62
  psychological problems and, 95–96
  SAT scores and, 30–31
  school achievement and, 77, 78–100, 131, 155–62, 185–87
  segregation and, 157, 159
  socializing and, 180–81, 182
  in student commitment study sample, 20–23, 78
  suicide rates and, 94–95
  teachers' bias and, 88–89
ETS (Educational Testing Service), 42, 43, 44
extracurricular activities, 18, 24, 125, 173–82
  ethnicity and, 180–82
  reexamination of, 192–93
  school achievement affected by, 174–77, 188
  time spent on, 174, 175–76, 180, 193
  varieties of, 173
extrinsic motivation, 72–74

failure:
    perceived causes of success and, 91–94
    perceived consequences of, 75, 76,
        90–91, 185–86
family breakdown, 13, 24
firmness vs. leniency, of parents, 106, 107,
    108–11, 112, 113
Fordham, Signithia, 160
Forrest Gump, 44
friendships:
    best, 139, 140
    children's achievements affected by,
        147–49, 160; *see also* peers

gender, grades and, 86
Georgia, University of, 160
Germany, 172
glass-ceiling hypothesis, school achieve-
    ment and, 89–91
"going through the motions," 67, 74
grade level, NAEP data and, 34
grades, 76
    "acceptable" levels of, 19, 128, 156,
       161
    divorce and, 86
    ethnicity and, 84–85, 135
    as extrinsic motivation, 73–74
    gender and, 86
    need to increase importance of, 189–90
    personal identification with, 93
    see also school achievement
graduation, seen as more important than
    learning, 75
"greasers," 144

"hands-on" learning, "book" learning vs.,
    173
happiness, 179
    as permissive parents' goal, 113–14
healthy achievement attributional styles,
    91–94
Hershey, Pa., 11–12
Hershey Chronicle, 11–12
Hispanics, *see* Latinos
home environment, *see* authoritative par-
    enting; parenting; parents
homework, 18

assigned amounts of, 66, 69, 179
ethnicity and, 87, 156, 185
immigrant students and, 97
parental involvement with, 125, 127
students' ignoring of, 69
time spent on, 19, 66, 67, 68, 70, 97,
    156, 173, 185
humanities, 33
Hungary, 179

ignorance, as celebrated trait, 44–45
immigrants, effects of Americanization
    on, 96–100
independence, obedience vs., 108
Indochinese refugee families, 88
indulgent (permissive) parenting, 112,
    113–14, 116, 117–18, 120
influence:
    parental vs. peer, 148, 151–52
    of peers, 25, 140–43
inner-city schools, 13, 21, 34, 53, 87–88,
    189
instructional methods, 48
"intellectuals," 144, 145
intelligence, 87
    achievement and, 65
    increased levels of, 65
    nature vs. nurture and, 58–60, 92–93
internalization, 110
intimacy, of peers, 139–40
intrinsic motivation, 72–74
IQ, 59

Japan, 36, 51, 179, 191
    student suicide rates in, 94–95
"jocks," 27, 144, 158

knowledge, parents' lack of, 103–4
Koretz, Dan, 46

Labor Department, U.S., 166
labor laws, child, 166, 167, 193
Latinos:
    achievement attribution and, 92
    Americanization and, 98, 185
    consequences of failing as perceived by,
       90–91

low school achievement of, 79, 82–85, 87–91, 99–100, 131, 155–62, 185, 190–91
parental disengagement and, 134*n*
parenting styles and, 133, 135
parents' language barrier and, 130
in student commitment study, 21, 78, 80
varied geographic and cultural backgrounds of, 80
launch trajectory, 149–50, 162
laws, child labor, 166, 167, 193
learning:
    ability, social and emotional influences on learning vs., 64–66
    "book" vs. "hands-on," 173
Learning Gap, The (Stevenson and Stigler), 41–42
leisure time of students, international comparisons of, 173
leniency vs. firmness, of parents, 106, 107, 108–11, 112, 113
liberals, school reform approach of, 48, 51–54, 57, 194
London, 50
"loners," 144
Losing Generations, 53
Lou Harris survey firm, 119

McNeil, Linda, 69
Maine, 193
marijuana, 150–51, 171
"Married . . . with Children," 44
math scores, 32, 33, 35, 36, 37
maturity, authoritative parents' fostering of, 113–14, 118, 123–24
media:
    Black identity as reflected in, 160
    inner-city problems emphasized by, 13, 34
    portrayals of adolescents in, 12–13, 62
Metropolitan Life Insurance Company, 119–20
Michael, Robert T., 44
Michigan, University of, 36, 95
Middle Eastern students, 80

minorities:
    as percentage of adolescent population, 78
    see also Asian-Americans; Blacks; ethnicity; Latinos; Whites
motivation:
    altering of, 77
    intrinsic vs. extrinsic, 72–74
    see also disengagement; engagement
movies, 44
"My So-Called Life," 13

National Academy of Sciences, 53
National Adult Literacy Study, 40
National Assessment of Educational Progress (NAEP), 32–35, 48, 49, 52
National Center for Education Statistics, 37, 39
National Education Commission on Time and Learning, 55
National Standards in American Education (Ravitch), 29–30, 190, 191
Nation at Risk, A, 36, 37–38, 42, 47
nature vs. nurture, school achievement and, 58–60, 92–93
neighborhoods, school achievement and, 152–54
"nerds," 144
New York Times, 94
nonacademic school activities, 55–56, 66, 68, 69
non-Hispanic Whites:
    definition of, 80
    see also Whites
nontraditional households, 105–6
normative standards, ethnicity and, 161–62

obedience:
    as authoritarian parents' goal, 113–14, 117
    independence vs., 108
obesity, 43
"off-task" time, 55
Ogbu, John, 160
"opportunities to learn," 48, 53, 57
opportunity, parents' lack of, 103, 105–6

Pacific Islanders, 80
parenting, 101–21, 122–37
  children's characteristics from different
    styles of, 116–18
  consistency of research on, 108–11
  cultural relativity and, 132–33
  effective, 132–33, 189
  ethnicity and, 131–37
  as learned skill, 103–4, 189
  in nontraditional households, 105–6
  school achievement and, 102–3,
    131–37
  styles of, 102–3, 111–14
  three fundamental dimensions of,
    106–8
  time requirements of, 105–6
  see also authoritarian parenting; author-
    itative parenting; permissive parent-
    ing
parents, 72, 101–21, 122–37
  acceptance vs. rejection by, 106–7,
    108–11, 112
  chief worries of, 179
  choice of schools made by, 48, 154–55
  consistency between, 115–16
  control vs. autonomy from, 106,
    107–11, 112–13
  disengagement of, 19–20, 118–21,
    133, 134n, 137, 142, 153, 187
  firmness vs. leniency of, 106, 107,
    108–11, 112, 113
  gap between intentions and actions of,
    103–6
  grade levels acceptable to, 19, 128,
    156, 161
  low standards set by, 69
  peer influence compared with, 148,
    151–52
  school involvement by, 124–26, 128–
    131, 189
  student commitment study and, 23–24
  three ways school achievement is af-
    fected by, 102–3
"partyers," 19, 158
peers, 24, 27, 72, 117–18, 137, 138–62
  amount of time spent with, 68
  ethnicity and, 144, 155–62

  influence of, 25, 140–43
  neighborhoods and, 152–54
  parental influence compared with, 148,
    151–52
  positive vs. negative influence of,
    142–43
  school achievement influenced by, 19,
    145–49, 155–62, 187–88
  school choice and, 154–55
  sorting process and, 149–52
  in student commitment study, 143,
    144–45
  three concentric circles of, 138–40
  various divisions of, 143–45
  see also socializing
permissive (indulgent) parenting, 112,
    113–14, 116, 117–18, 120
Philadelphia, Pa., 38
Phillips, Layli, 160
play time, 178
"populars," 143–44, 158
"preppies," 144
preschoolers, 73
private schools, 22, 154, 155
psychological functioning, 25–26, 95–96,
    98
  authoritative parenting and, 116–18,
    123–24
  parental disengagement and, 119–20
  parental style and, 116–18
psychology courses, 40
public service television announcements,
    student-produced, 130–31

race:
  use of term, 79
  see also ethnicity
Ravitch, Diane, 29–30, 31, 190, 191
reading:
  college freshmen levels of, 38
  for pleasure, 19, 164
  test scores in, 32, 33, 35
Reagan administration, 47
refugee families, 88
rejection vs. acceptance, by parents,
    106–7, 108–11, 112
remedial courses, 38–39, 41, 77, 192

responsibility, sense of, 109
responsive parenting, *see* authoritative parenting
rural schools, 21, 84

Scholastic Aptitude Tests (SAT), 192
    declining scores on, 30–31, 32, 33, 34, 36, 37, 42, 45, 48–49
    recentering of, 42–44
school achievement, 29–46
    achievement attribution and, 91–94, 98, 124
    after-school employment and, 19, 25, 69, 169–71
    Americanization and, 96–100, 185
    authoritative parenting and, 122–23, 126–27, 133
    changing the consequences of failure in, 76
    class difference and, 79, 81, 83, 86
    consequences of decline in, 37–41
    denial of decline in, 41–44, 45–46, 183–84
    ethnicity and, 77, 78–100, 131, 155–62, 185–87
    extracurricular activities and, 174–77, 188
    glass-ceiling hypothesis and, 89–91
    glorification of stupidity and, 44–45
    intelligence and, 65
    international comparisons of, 35–37, 49, 56–57, 94, 163
    later success predicted by, 16
    as national priority, 188–89
    national standards for, 190–91
    nature vs. nurture and, 58–60, 92–93
    neighborhoods and, 152–54
    nonacademic school content as response to decline in, 55–56
    parents' effect on, 102–3, 131–37
    peer group influence on, 19, 145–49, 155–62, 187–88
    school quality and, 49–51, 57–58, 83–84, 87–88
    socializing and, 177–79, 180–82
    sports activities and, 19
    statewide comparisons of, 20
    students' belief in consequences of failure in, 75, 76, 90–91, 185–86
    students' belief in eventual payoff of, 74–75, 89–91, 97, 186
    ten recommendations for improvement in, 188–93
    see also grades; standardized achievement tests
school calendar, 48
    protest over, 11–12
school day, length of, 66, 173, 177, 179–80
school orientation, 71
school reform, 47–61
    conservative approach to, 48, 54–57, 69, 194
    liberal approach to, 48, 51–54, 57, 194
    as political agenda, 47–48
    schools vs. students' lives as focus of, 48, 57–58, 60–61, 63, 184, 188, 194
schools:
    inner-city, 13, 21, 34, 53, 87–88, 189
    low demands made on students in, 66, 67, 68, 70, 76
    as misplaced focus of proposed reform, 48, 57–58, 60–61, 63, 184, 188, 194
    nonacademic activities in, 55–56, 66, 68, 69
    parental involvement at, 124–26, 128–131, 189
    parents' choice of, 48, 154–55
    private, 22, 154, 155
    rural, 21, 84
    school achievement and, 49–51, 57–58, 83–84, 87–88
    social problems addressed through, 53–54
    in student commitment study, 20–23, 84
schools choice debate, 154–55
school transcripts, national standards for, 191–92
science scores, 32, 33, 35, 36, 37
segregation, 157, 159
self-control, 109

self-esteem, 17, 109, 110, 116, 117, 120, 179

Sex in America (Michael), 44

sexual precocity, 17, 44, 63, 121, 187

"Simpsons, The," 44

skill, parents' lack of, 103, 104–5

social competence, 109, 114, 116, 117, 120, 144

socializing:
    ethnicity and, 180–81, 182
    school achievement and, 177–79, 180–82

social mobility, 158

Spanish language, 130

sports activities, 173, 193
    school achievement affected by, 19, 175–77

standardized achievement tests, 13, 64, 65
    see also National Assessment of Educational Progress; Scholastic Aptitude Tests

Stanford University, 14

Stevenson, Harold, 36, 41–42

Stigler, James, 41–42

student commitment study, 13–28
    adolescents as focus of, 17–18
    description of, 13–14
    design overview of, 195–201
    ethnic classification system used in, 79–82
    ethnic diversity of sample in, 20–23, 78
    findings of, 18–20
    focus groups and personal interviews used in, 27–28
    goals of, 13, 15
    means of collecting data used in, 26–27
    peer groups in, 143, 144–45
    students' home lives studied in, 23–24
    students' lives outside home studied in, 24–26
    time line of, 26

stupidity, glorification of, 44–45

suburban schools, 13, 21, 84

success, perceived causes of failure and, 91–94

suicide, 121, 187
    ethnicity and, 94–95

system-work, 127

Taiwan, 36, 179

teachers, 13, 40
    ethnic bias and, 88–89
    "off-task" time spent by, 55
    ratio of students to, 39
    salaries of, 55
    selection and training of, 48
    student employment and, 69

teenagers, *see* adolescents; peers

television:
    portrayals of adolescents on, 12–13
    student-produced public service announcements for, 130–31
    stupidity glorified on, 44–45
    viewing time spent on, 177–78

Temple University, 14, 40, 159

territory, peer, 149, 150–51, 162

track assignment, 89

transcripts, national standards for, 191–192

"trouble threshold," 161

two-year colleges, 192

underachievers, 123, 146
    economic costs of, 37–41

unhealthy achievement attributional styles, 91–94

universities, 84
    effects of incoming low achieving students on, 38–41
    raising entrance requirements of, 76–77
    remedial courses at, 38–39, 41, 77, 192

verbal test scores, 32

violations, curfew, 113–14

vouchers, school choice, 154–55

Washington, 193

Wayne's World, 44

Western Europe, 172, 173

Whites:
    achievement attribution and, 92
    parenting styles and, 133, 135, 136–137
    peer group access of, 158
    SAT scores and, 31

school achievement of, 83, 84, 131
in student commitment study, 21,
    80
Wisconsin, 20, 84
Wisconsin, University of, 14

work ethic, 93–94
working the system, 127
work orientation, 70–71
writing ability, 38, 40–41
writing scores, 32, 33–34, 35

DATE DUE
